To John

a staunc_

Tic, and good friend.

Gerry Nov/97.

IN PURSUIT OF
BRITISH INTERESTS

By the same author

EXPERIENCES OF CHINA

IN PURSUIT OF BRITISH INTERESTS

Reflections on Foreign Policy
under Margaret Thatcher
and John Major

———

PERCY CRADOCK

JOHN MURRAY
Albemarle Street, London

First published in 1997
by John Murray (Publishers) Ltd,
50 Albemarle Street, London W1X 4BD

A catalogue record for this book is available from
the British Library

ISBN 0-7195-5464 0

Typeset in 12/14pt Garamond by
Servis Filmsetting Ltd, Manchester
Printed and bound in Great Britain by
The University Press, Cambridge

To Birthe

Contents

Contents

Illustrations

The author and publisher wish to acknowledge the following for permission to reproduce illustrations: Plates 1 and 3, Associated Press; 2, Tass; 4, Times Newspapers; 5, Rex Features; 6 and 9, Camera Press; 7, Press Association; 8, Reuters.

Acknowledgements

I SHOULD LIKE to acknowledge the help I have had from friends and former colleagues in writing this book. Lord Thomas, Sir Leslie Fielding and Professor Peter Hennessy were kind enough to read the text and make valuable corrections and suggestions. Sir Robin Renwick, on South Africa, and Sir Peter Hall, on Yugoslavia, allowed me to draw on their special knowledge. I had a stimulating general talk with Sir Charles Powell: we agreed over wide areas and agreed to differ over others.

I have also had much help from Simon Blundell, the librarian of the Reform Club, from the staff of the London Library and the Reading Room of the British Library and from Fiona Meiklejohn of *The Times* Picture Library over illustrations.

Douglas Matthews has ensured that, whatever else it lacks, the book has an authoritative index.

As always, I am happy to acknowledge my debt to my editor, Gail Pirkis.

'Therefore, I say that it is a narrow policy to suppose that this country or that is to be marked out as the eternal ally or the perpetual enemy of England. Our interests are eternal and perpetual, and those interests it is our duty to follow.'

Lord Palmerston, House of Commons, 1 March 1848

'If men could learn from history, what lessons it might teach us! But passion and party blind our eyes, and the light which experience gives us is a lantern on the stern, which shines only on the waves behind us!'

Coleridge, from T. Allsop, *Recollections*, 1831

Introduction

THIS BOOK HAS its origins in the eight and a half years I spent at 10 Downing Street, from 1984 to 1992, as the Prime Minister's Foreign Policy Adviser under Margaret Thatcher and John Major. In that long assignment, and in the questions I have since asked myself on the nature of our diplomacy in those years and its effectiveness. It is an attempt to give some impressions of British foreign policy in an eventful period and to reach some judgements on it in the light of later reflection.

I visited one corner of the ground, policy toward China and Hong Kong, in a book I wrote on that subject three years ago.[1] This is in many ways a less easy and obvious work than its predecessor. The China story wrote itself. It had a unity of theme: we were looking throughout at one canvas, however large and obscure. Here there is a multiplicity of subjects, the general flux of international affairs. In the case of China I was a central player and could write with authority. In this, though I saw and advised on much of the action, there were a number of influences at work and often I was simply one voice among several. It is therefore a more diffuse and less reliable account.

Is it worth attempting? There are cautionary voices. Indolence. The difficulty, lacking access to confidential papers, of recalling what took place some years ago. The conventions of official retirement. Though we now have rather more open government, the Official Secrets Act is very much alive and these cautious pages will still have to struggle past the censors. And though the position of civil servants has changed and ministers are readier than they once were to distribute responsibility to officials, I suspect they still prefer to keep the memoirs field to themselves, expecting their advisers to maintain a respectful silence. So history is left to form, the product of the self-justification of the politicians and the half-knowledge of the journalists. And most officials are content to leave it so.

On the other hand the events of those years, and the British contribution to them, were remarkable by any standards: the Thatcher-Reagan relationship; Gorbachev; the collapse of the Soviet empire; the controversies over Europe; German reunification; the transformation of South Africa; the Gulf War. They have shaped our present environment, our problems and opportunities. To have been involved in such happenings and to have advised on our responses was a privilege and at the same time an insight into the way British government worked and British policy was formed. There is a natural temptation to set something down, and even, it could be argued, an historical obligation to do so. Such a memoir would give personal satisfaction, not the least of considerations. It could be useful eventually as a small addition to the archive on the years which the future historian might label in dynastic terms as late Thatcher and early Major. Above all, it would have a bearing on current issues, on Britain's present foreign policy predicament. But, for the work to be done and have such relevance, it would have to be done now; and I should have to risk the reproach that, even at seventy-three, I was rushing into print.

It is on this admittedly narrow balance of advantage that I have decided to write. I hope readers will agree that it was worth doing so.

Since this is a less personal narrative than the China book, I have adopted a different format. In the first section I describe the framework within which work was done and policy made, the physical setting, the organization and the personalities concerned. In the second I give a roughly chronological commentary on foreign policy under the main subject headings, the United States, the

Soviet Union, Europe and the like. I do not pretend to be exhaustive: it is a commentary not a history. I have assumed a certain degree of knowledge on the part of the reader; there are also sizeable omissions: Ireland, for example, is too domestic and is only touched on; the full Yugoslav tragedy came after my time and only the beginnings are covered; as explained above, detail on China is to be found elsewhere. There may also be a certain weighting in the direction of drama and trouble: the more undemanding relations, however fruitful, the steady diplomatic or commercial intercourse which holds the world together and forms the background for the crises, these tend to take second place. But the main themes are here; also one that is less common. Since during most of the time, as well as being the Foreign Policy Adviser, I also chaired the Joint Intelligence Committee, I add a chapter on intelligence and policy.

In the final section I attempt a judgement on how successful our policies were in those years, how far they secured British interests and whether they offer any lessons for the future. This has called for a certain detachment from them, a willingness to allow that some were better conceived than others. This will be controversial. But without such detachment, it is impossible to attempt serious history, or intelligent discussion of Britain's present place in the world.

I have drawn mainly on memory, helped by notes made at the time. But I have naturally studied the accounts given by the leading players as well as the public records. I have also consulted one or two friends and former colleagues. I am greatly indebted to them for their help, without which this book would be much poorer and less accurate, though I have to stress that its judgements and its errors are entirely my own.

PERCY CRADOCK
September 1996

Part I

The Setting

I

An Offer not to be Refused

I WAS INVITED to become Margaret Thatcher's Foreign Policy Adviser in September 1983. There was a surprise telephone call from John Coles, her Private Secretary. I am afraid I responded with less enthusiasm than the splendid offer deserved. I was at the time Ambassador to China, deep in the Hong Kong negotiations and only briefly back in London for consultation. I also had a shrewd idea that on leaving Peking I could be offered the post of Chairman of the Joint Intelligence Committee when Sir Antony Duff retired in late 1984. I knew about this post from earlier service in the Cabinet Office and was attracted by it.

But my main reason for doubt about John Coles's proposition was an acute sense of the patchiness of my foreign affairs experience: on that slender base I could not possibly aspire to be a universal guru. I added, in words which must have seemed a little naïve to my future employers, and which would in the light of later events acquire an ironic quality, that the Prime Minister already had a perfectly good foreign policy adviser in the shape of Sir Geoffrey Howe, the new Foreign Secretary.

In view of these doubts I was asked to call on Sir Anthony Parsons, the incumbent Foreign Policy Adviser, and it was rapidly borne in on me that the decision was made. He was to bow out at Christmas and I was to take his place. There was a brief interview with the Prime Minister herself, a sort of laying-on of hands, my hesitations were brushed aside, and the matter was settled.

Mrs Thatcher had acquired her first Foreign Policy Adviser at the beginning of 1983 in the light of her disenchantment with the Foreign Office as a result of the Falklands experience. She wanted a senior figure on her personal staff who would alert her to coming problems and if need be offer independent advice. An obvious choice was Tony Parsons, our Ambassador at the United Nations, who in the early days of the Falklands crisis had distinguished himself by lining up a decisive majority in the Security Council, condemning Argentine aggression, and providing an unassailable legal basis for our future operations.

Tony, a Middle East specialist by upbringing, highly articulate, confident, down-to-earth and outgoing, had established a good, not too deferential, relationship with the Prime Minister and had begun to invent the job he held as he went along. (There were no terms of reference.) But he only came up to London three days a week and he was anxious to retire to his house in the West Country, to lecture at Exeter University and to write. A replacement was urgently needed.

Foreign affairs advisers at No. 10 have a bad name in the Foreign Office. They have existed rarely and usually at inauspicious times. The title conjures up the ill-omened figure of Sir Horace Wilson, translated by Baldwin from the Ministry of Labour to No. 10, there to become Neville Chamberlain's most active collaborator in the appeasement of Germany in the late 1930s. More generally, it spells divided authority and the possibility that No. 10 could rival or displace the Foreign Office in the direction of foreign policy.

Prime ministers, as they grow more experienced and confident, invariably move in on this area. Under Lloyd George at the end of the First World War, the tendency was particularly pronounced and a contemporary article spoke of foreign policy 'growing like Topsy in the sanctities of No. 10 Downing Street out of the brains of miscellaneous informants and secretaries'.[2]

Philip Kerr (later Lord Lothian), Lloyd George's Private Secretary, was given special licence at the time. One story has Balfour, then Foreign Secretary, asking him whether Lloyd George had read a particular memorandum. 'I don't think so,' said Kerr, 'but I have.' 'Not quite the same thing is it, Philip – yet?' said Balfour.

Much later, under Harold Macmillan, a more orthodox Prime Minister but also a foreign policy activist, Philip de Zulueta, another Private Secretary, was also highly influential. And there had been recurrent complaints, from foreign secretaries as diverse as Lord Curzon and George Brown, that policy was being taken out of their hands by the Prime Minister.

Alive to these precedents and to the danger that the Foreign Policy Adviser might burgeon on the American model into a National Security Adviser, complete with staff, the Foreign Office devised a set of self-denying ordinances, which the Adviser was invited to sign. For the most part they were sensible arrangements to avoid the crossing of wires, like the undertakings not to make a habit of receiving foreign ambassadors and not to cultivate the press. Since I had no time or inclination to do either I was content to sign the articles, and relations with the Foreign Office were soon on an amicable footing.

The Ministry of Defence reacted more brutally to the new situation. A Defence Adviser was also appointed in early 1983. But Michael Heseltine, the Defence Secretary, simply forbade Ministry staff to take his telephone calls. The Defence Adviser found himself frozen out. He was soon withdrawn, and advice on defence issues at No. 10 was subsumed in the Foreign Policy Adviser's portfolio.

In fact, these fears of a new empire, a Prime Minister's Department in the full sense, were exaggerated if only because of characteristic British parsimony over resources and the British preference for hand-to-mouth arrangements. The Treasury kept a beady eye on the size of the No. 10 establishment, and Mrs Thatcher's housekeeping instincts ran along the same lines. The Foreign Policy Adviser found he had a secretary to type his minutes and little else.

He was also never quite full-time. Tony Parsons worked a three-day week. I was there every day, but was required to do two jobs. For the first year I was also a Deputy Under-Secretary in the

Foreign Office responsible for the Hong Kong negotiations. After the signature of the Joint Declaration, from 1985 until 1992, I was also Chairman of the Joint Intelligence Committee with wide responsibilities for British intelligence. There were always two offices, two in-trays, two piles of papers. Under those conditions, if there was to be a contest with the hundreds of high-powered operators across the road in the Foreign Office, it was going to be a very unequal one.

The Adviser's responsibilities, as Tony Parsons and I worked them out, could be defined as, first, to anticipate crises and see that the Prime Minister was briefed in advance of having to take quick decisions on Foreign Office recommendation; and second, to interpret to the Foreign Office what was in the Prime Minister's mind in the field of international relations. For this, regular liaison was needed. I was in continuous contact with senior Foreign Office officials and also had weekly meetings to run over the agenda with the Permanent Under-Secretary, Sir Antony Acland, later Sir Patrick Wright. There were rarer meetings with the Foreign Secretary.

The third function was to offer the Prime Minister independent advice on important issues. This did not mean automatic disagreement with the Foreign Secretary; but it did ensure a second opinion, and a check for the Prime Minister that the official advice she was receiving was the best calculated to promote our interests.

To enable me to convey this advice I received a copy of all the Foreign Office telegrams sent to the Private Secretary at No. 10 and all inter-departmental correspondence on foreign and defence issues. I attended all ministerial meetings on these subjects, with the exception of the Cabinet, and as a participant rather than a scribe.

The exception of the Cabinet was less important than it might seem. In Mrs Thatcher's time the Cabinet rarely debated foreign policy, as distinct from hearing reports of decisions taken. The usual level of decision was, formally, at Cabinet committee – the Overseas and Defence Committee – and in practice at small *ad hoc* groups of ministers and advisers, the Prime Minister's preferred way of working.

I also had private meetings with the Prime Minister as occasion required, on specific issues and, at regular intervals, for more general surveys. I sat in on many of her meetings with foreign visitors. I also wrote her many minutes.

I did not, however, attempt to interpose myself in the regular stream of official correspondence between ministries and No. 10. That was a matter for the private offices. Decisions by the Prime Minister, even if resulting from some proposal I had made, were to be recorded through the proper channels, again by the Private Secretary. It had to be made clear that I was an adviser and not an executant; I could influence decisions, but they had to be reached and recorded in the regular way.

Nor did I attempt to travel regularly with the Prime Minister. In practice this could not easily be done because of the demands of my second post. It would also have raised awkward questions in the Prime Minister's meetings with her hosts. The Private Secretary had to attend to take the record. The British Ambassador on the spot had a prior claim to be there as the Queen's representative. If the Foreign Secretary was also in the visiting party he was hard to exclude (though he was on occasion). The stage army grew; and the Prime Minister's strong preference was for meetings restricted to the principals and a note-taker. The decision not to accompany her affected both visibility and influence, but it seemed to me inescapable.

I travelled on official business regularly to Washington to exchange notes with the National Security Adviser, the head of the CIA and senior officials in the State Department; much less frequently to Europe; and on occasion to China, Japan and the Soviet Union. But, with rare exceptions, these were journeys on my own, not in the Prime Minister's train.

2

Advisers and Secretaries

No. 10 DOWNING STREET is a deceptive building. The front is undistinguished, one of a row of late seventeenth-century houses put up by a speculative builder. But once inside, the prospect widens. A broad corridor leads to what was another much grander house, once the home of the Hanoverian envoy to the court of Queen Anne, later redesigned by William Kent and given to Walpole by George II as the official residence of the First Lord of the Treasury. Here is the Cabinet room and the main staircase, lined with portraits of former first ministers, rising to the state rooms on the first floor. The building contains a modest flat for the Prime Minister and, surprisingly, retains something of the atmosphere of a private house. But my memory of it is of a warren filled with offices, small units covering various aspects of the Prime Minister's responsibilities, the political office, the honours section, the press office and so on.

The caretaker's flat on the second floor had been transformed in this way to accommodate advisers. The Foreign Policy Adviser had a handsome room with windows giving on to Horse Guards Parade, whence in the summer months inspiriting music would rise as the Guards marched and countermarched rehearsing the Trooping of the Colour.

The next-door room was occupied by Alan Walters, the Economic Adviser, on his rare appearances. Across the corridor was the Policy Unit, a group advising on domestic issues, in my time under John Redwood, then Brian Griffiths and finally Sarah Hogg. And of course our secretarial staff.

But the centre of operations lay below, in the two rooms on the ground floor adjoining the Cabinet room and occupied by the private secretaries. One room housed the Principal Private Secretary, the official head of the Prime Minister's household, seconded from the Treasury, and the Private Secretary covering foreign affairs, seconded from the Foreign Office. The larger room held three more private secretaries, seconded from home departments, covering economic, home and parliamentary affairs, a diary secretary and a duty clerk.

My main concern was with the foreign affairs Private Secretary, who represented access to the Prime Minister and who was the only other official concerned with international issues in No. 10. By virtue of his office he stood as close to the Prime Minister as it was possible to get: like his colleagues from other departments, he was with her or on call throughout her working day, taking a note of her discussions, recording her decisions, drafting her letters and, in part at least, her speeches, commissioning and editing the Foreign Office briefs prepared for her, and in general controlling the interminable flow of official correspondence. It was an intensely demanding and responsible position and automatically conferred great influence. For the secretary was not only a conduit; unavoidably he was to some degree an adviser, the degree depending on the character of the Prime Minister and the official in question. The precedents of Philip Kerr, Philip de Zulueta and many others less prominent or notorious were there to underline the point.

The officials appointed to this post were hand-picked, the most able, industrious and discreet the Foreign Office could provide. Those I dealt with easily maintained or surpassed this high standard. John Coles, who was there when I arrived, and who went on to become Ambassador to Jordan, High Commissioner to Australia, and finally Permanent Under-Secretary at the Foreign Office, impressed me by the calm, almost priest-like, with which he discharged his multifarious functions and managed, if that is the right word, his demanding mistress. I had the highest respect for him.

His successor, Charles Powell, was a rather different character, and since he has a prominent role in any account of Mrs Thatcher's ministry he deserves more extended notice. I knew Charles well: he had worked for me in 1969 and 1970 when I was head of the Foreign Office Planning Staff, and I had sent him off with my best recommendation to be Private Secretary to Lord Cromer, our Ambassador in Washington. I warmly approved his appointment to No. 10 which, Geoffrey Howe tells us, could as easily have been to his own private office.

Charles was immensely well endowed for the work: a sharp intelligence; a remarkable facility for drafting and encapsulating the sense of a discussion in clear, unambiguous words; great speed and ease at transacting business generally; high linguistic ability; and intense industry – he would be at his desk from six in the morning until late at night. But he was courtier as well as clerk, possessing an easy, engaging manner, an ability to recommend himself in a variety of settings, and a well-developed sense of humour. He was ambitious; he was of the world and flourished in it. Above all, he had the ability to sense the wishes of the Prime Minister and to convey her views. His own and hers were often indistinguishable.

In the memoirs of Saint-Simon, whose picture of Louis XIV's court sometimes casts light on the activities in Mrs Thatcher's immediate circle, there is an account of how Rose, one of the King's private secretaries, 'held the pen'. Saint-Simon says he was 'a kind of public forger', imitating the King's handwriting so perfectly that he could thereby relieve Louis of writing all manner of letters. The King signed Rose's letters with his own hand, and the handwriting of the rest was so much like his own that no one could have discerned the least difference.

It was sometimes equally difficult to establish where Mrs Thatcher ended and Charles Powell began. Perhaps it could be said that for some years he 'held the pen'. Saint-Simon goes on to comment that 'among the four private secretaries the one who holds the pen has all the privileges and the others have none except their entrées'.

These abilities and activities, however, did not entirely accord with civil service norms. For example, Charles frequently over-stepped the line between the official and the political domains. He also had a flair for publicity. The rule was, and is, that private secretaries should be self-effacing and avoid the press. Charles on the other hand seemed to enjoy the most fruitful relations with them. After some time I was surprised to read in the newspapers profiles of him under the heading of the Prime Minister's Foreign Policy Adviser, a title he seemed to prefer to that of Private Secretary. This was tiresome but, in the end, not serious. What was important was that the Prime Minister's business was done, and well done. The way the public credits were distributed was secondary. We were both necessary and our co-operation critical.

To the Foreign Office, however, his employers, and to the Cabinet Office in the person of the Cabinet Secretary, Charles began to present a more formidable problem. His closeness to the Prime Minister and his influence with her, his willingness to venture into the political world, came to be seen as a threat to the balance between No. 10 and Whitehall and even to the constitutional division between ministers and civil servants. It certainly accentuated rather than relieved the strains between No. 10 and the Foreign Office. Charles and the Press Secretary, Bernard Ingham, portrayed as Mrs Thatcher's praetorian guard or, by those less well disposed, as the Ratcliffe and Catesby of a tyrannical ruler, underlined the dangerous dominance, and loneliness, of their mistress. Ministers and Members of Parliament as well as officials came to resent their influence. It was clearly time for a change of staff.

But how was this to be accomplished? The custom is that after two to three years at the centre, the Private Secretary returns to his department, is promoted and passes back into the stream of diplomatic life. Charles, however, proved impossible to move. A series of desperate conferences was held between Sir Robin Butler and Sir Patrick Wright, the Foreign Office Permanent Under-Secretary. A series of embassies was proposed, in ascending order. First Berne, then Madrid; in the end there were even whispers of Washington. But there were no takers. Mrs Thatcher would not let him go and he stayed with her until she fell.

Charles Powell's answer to these charges would have been that, while at No. 10, he owed his loyalty to the Prime Minister. Certainly he served her well and she was grateful. In that ungenerous book, *The Downing Street Years*, she sadly omits any mention of her other Foreign Office private secretaries. But she devotes a special passage of praise to his help; and the praise is deserved.

My own relations with this exceptional private secretary were from the outset extremely friendly and, despite minor frictions, remained so. We were in constant contact. However unhealthy the situation from a constitutional point of view, it appeared to be the way the Prime Minister wanted her work done and there was more than enough for the two of us. In some areas, such as Europe, he was more active. In others, the Far East and to some extent the Soviet Union, I took the lead. Happily, our views were often close.

Here, in order to prevent misunderstandings, it would be right to note some of the other sources of advice, outside the Foreign Office, available to the Prime Minister on international issues. On European Community matters, there was a powerful unit sited in the Cabinet Office under David Williamson and later Michael Jay. They provided the detailed briefing for Community ministerial meetings in Brussels or elsewhere. Again in the Cabinet Office there was the Deputy Under-Secretary in the Cabinet Secretariat, the select group of officials who record discussions in Cabinet and in Cabinet committees. The Deputy Secretary, traditionally seconded from the Foreign Office, was a senior official who, in addition to his secretarial duties, had a co-ordinating role where advice on international questions involving a number of departments was required. He would chair *ad hoc* groups of colleagues from the Foreign Office, the Ministry of Defence and other ministries, and would submit his recommendations via the Cabinet Secretary. In my time the post was held by Bryan Cartledge, later Ambassador in Moscow, David Goodall, later High Commissioner in New Delhi, Christopher Mallaby, later Ambassador in Bonn and Paris, Len Appleyard, later Ambassador in Peking, and Pauline Neville-Jones, who refused the Embassy in Bonn to take up a business appointment.

Finally there was the Cabinet Secretary himself, the distillation of official wisdom. To one Cabinet Secretary, Sir Robert Armstrong, and his deputy, David Goodall, were due the official credits for the Anglo-Irish Agreement of 1985.

The advice the Prime Minister received on a particular issue was therefore often an amalgam: a brief perhaps from the Foreign Office, or a minute from the Cabinet Office, summarized with comments by the Private Secretary, a minute from the Foreign Policy Adviser, all in her overnight box. Then, if there was to be a ministerial meeting, there might be a chance of a word or two with her beforehand.

At the meeting, if it was a Cabinet committee, the Cabinet Secretary and his deputy would be there and would be responsible for the record. If, as happened more often, it was an *ad hoc* group, there would be one or two ministers, the Private Secretary and myself. The Private Secretary took the record.

Outside Whitehall there was guidance available from the Centre for Policy Studies, on which Mrs Thatcher had relied greatly in her earlier years. Alfred Sherman, its former Director of Studies, still communicated with her and in my early days at No. 10 used to come to see me from time to time. Wise and usually less extreme advice came from Hugh Thomas, the head of the Centre. They or others would offer ideas or be asked for drafts for speeches. Individual experts could be called in, Robert Conquest on the Soviet Union, or Michael Butler on the European Community.

But the catchment area was broader still. The Prime Minister had a wide circle of friends, and foreign policy is not seen as a particularly arcane subject: everyone has a view on what the foreigners are up to. I often had to encounter judgements which, channelled through the Prime Minister, acquired considerable force but which originated from unnamed and highly unorthodox sources. China and Hong Kong, I found, were a fertile field for amateur advisers.

From time to time the Prime Minister also held seminars at Chequers on international issues, drawing on academic experts as well as ministers and officials. The Foreign Policy Adviser and Private Secretary between them were supposed to organize and script such occasions. Some of them became famous. One, just before my time, inaugurated a more open approach to Eastern Europe and led eventually to the first meeting with Gorbachev. The content of another, on Germany in March 1990, was leaked, to general embarrassment.

It was very much to the Prime Minister's credit that she found time for these gatherings and deliberately raised her sights from the day-to-day action. Although not perhaps a thinker herself, she had a respect for ideas and for those who purveyed them, in the same way that she had an old-fashioned respect, perhaps derived from her father, for learning and for holders of first-class degrees from ancient universities. She also found the academics a useful foil to the Foreign Office and took pleasure in praising the first to the detriment of the second.

3

The Prime Minister

WHATEVER HER INNOCENCE of foreign affairs when she took over in 1979, by the time I came to work for her Mrs Thatcher was already an experienced stateswoman. She had met, and argued with, most of the world's leaders. She had established a warm relationship with President Reagan and had fought successfully against the European Community to lower Britain's contributions and recover her money, as she put it. The defining experience of the Falklands War was behind her. There was greater fame to come but broadly she knew what she wanted. The main lineaments were there, the bone structure perhaps not so sharply defined as in later years, but clearly visible: the belief in strong defence, the instinctive alignment with the United States, the anti-Communism, the suspicion of Europe, the tireless assertion of British interests, as she defined those entities.

She was well informed, had read many Foreign Office papers and absorbed a high proportion of them. She had a good memory, particularly of things one would have preferred her to forget. Her industry was outstanding: minutes and briefs came back thoroughly worked over, wavy lines in the margin indicating dissent, heavy underlining for the passages where she agreed. She took a special pride in mastering detail. She was neurotically punctual.

She could manage on only a few hours' sleep and spent almost all her waking hours at work. One of the earlier Rothschilds said of himself: 'I do not read books, I do not play cards, I do not go to the theatre, my only pleasure is my business.' She was not quite so single-minded, but almost so.

She went to the theatre or opera occasionally. She read thrillers and sometimes a book bearing on her political work – the life of Lord Liverpool, in deference to one predecessor who reigned even longer, a history of the Jews, in deference to her Jewish constituents in Finchley. There would be brief summer holidays, in Switzerland, Austria or England, again interspersed with official discussions or study of official reports; and if she was in England she was dangerously ready to reappear in Downing Street at the first hint of crisis.

In fact, she seemed happiest with her red boxes and one of my most abiding memories is of her coming down the steps from her flat to the study in Downing Street, exactly on time, beautifully turned out, with every sign of positive anticipation of a good discussion on some particularly ugly international situation.

Her mind was not remarkable in the academic sense: I have known many cleverer people; and the ideas were largely supplied by others. In fact she relied to a marked degree on emotion and instinct. But she was remarkable for the strength and tenacity of her views. She represented energy, courage and will. She was a natural force; and in a world which many found too complex for their liking she was often admired for the strength of her views, regardless of their substance. She satisfied a widespread and instinctive yearning for leadership, which at root was probably a nostalgia for past simplicities and days of greater British power.

She was different. It was partly that she carried with her into No. 10 a greater baggage of ideology than her predecessors. It was partly that she was a scientist by training, not, for once, a product of *litterae humaniores*. It was partly that she was a woman. The combination of femininity and power intrigued and excited her male interlocutors, from President Mitterrand to Anthony Powell. She was intensely feminine, making rapid, instinctive judgements on people, reacting well to certain kinds of men, and losing few opportunities of commenting on male weaknesses and inadequacies.

She was also intensely serious. The camaraderie, the relaxed, joky, allusive style, the affectation of doing things well without trying, the view of politics, and most other things, as a game, these expressions of the ruling male culture, which with Harold Macmillan had been carried to extreme lengths, all these were alien to her. She was exerting her full powers in matters of national importance and had no qualms about showing it. There was no time for amateurs. There were no jokes, apart from an occasional touch of hangman's humour. Nor could there be any relaxation on the part of those about her. I remember complaints from her that in a meeting with Judge Webster, the head of the CIA, when she had been making some very routine remarks, I had looked less than riveted.

She was clear and assertive, usually over-assertive, sometimes strident. No one was in doubt as to her position. She argued cogently. But she had little feeling for words, for the rhythms of the language. Speech-writing on her behalf was an ordeal from which I soon excused myself. By the second revision the phrases had lost their life; and the second revision was only the beginning of a grinding and soul-destroying process. A committee of drafters would labour through successive revisions into the small hours, by which time the language had died the death and no one cared any more which particular adjective was used.

By the same token, and more seriously, she had little sense of the forces moving the other side in international exchanges; of the history, the prejudices, the aspirations which drove her opposite numbers to adopt positions differing from her own but in their eyes equally valid; and of the overriding need to understand these forces, not as a prelude to a graceful surrender, but so as accurately to assess likely reactions to British moves and the strengths and weaknesses of opponents, or competitors, or partners. In other words, as a means of getting our way.

She had on the whole a poor view of foreigners, other than Anglo-Saxons, just as she had little time for European traditions or statesmen. This lack of imagination about the other side was a real defect. Too often it meant a one-dimensional policy, the assertion of British claims in a vacuum, with inevitable surprises and rebuffs when the other party failed to fit into our preconceptions. In a world in which we had long lost a dominant role and had increasingly to live by our wits, this was dangerous.

She tended to see foreign policy not as a continuum, the stream, largely beyond governments' control, on which, to use Bismarck's image, the powers are borne, but on which they can navigate with more or less skill, the stream on which Lord Salisbury would occasionally be moved to put out a punt pole to forestall a collision, but rather as a series of disparate problems with attainable solutions, or even as zero-sum games, which Britain had to win. She regularly complained that her advisers brought her problems but no answers. The thought that for a middling power in a disorderly world there would be few answers in the crossword-puzzle sense and many compromises seemed not to occur.

In a reflective passage in her memoirs she divides foreign policy questions into two kinds, those calling for urgent decision, and those where efforts at solutions will only make things worse. Statesmanship lies in the ability to distinguish the two. I have to say that in my experience with her I came across few examples of the 'wise impassivity' approach. The Daoist side of the Prime Minister was little in evidence. 'Action', or 'Action this day' was more the flavour of the time.

She looked for the radical, extreme course, something clear-cut and decisive. 'Wet' and 'waffly' were fatal judgements. If the line involved confrontation it was more likely to be sound. She was suspicious of nuances and accommodations. But, and here the political tactician took over from the ideologue, she was prepared to compromise under extreme persuasion, in order to achieve a practical result. In both the Rhodesia settlement and the Hong Kong agreement she retreated a long way from her original position and, very properly, claimed credit for the outcome. At the same time she reserved the right to repine privately and lament her concessions, thereby succeeding in having it both ways.

Discussion with her was demanding. She rarely followed a logical course, but would dart about from one aspect to another, making a series of assertions, delving into inconsequential detail, mixing routine or irrelevant comment with sudden *aperçus* which went to the heart of the matter, generating, it seemed almost deliberately, the maximum heat and confusion. It was as if she believed that nothing of value could emerge out of quiet reflection and logical exchanges; and that that way lay the dreaded 'consensus'. It was rather easier in small gatherings, where she felt less need to impose her style. But she always expected robust counter-argument; the obsequious approach was fatal. And success came, if ever, when the counter-arguments were registered and adopted, usually without attribution, after a short interval.

With her ministers she was rougher: the courtesies were reserved for her personal retainers. Churchill once said, I think jokingly, 'All I wanted was compliance with my wishes after reasonable discussion.' With her, there was often not even the prelude of reasonable discussion. She would begin a ministerial meeting by saying that she wanted to hear the views of X and Y, but wished first to make a few points of her own, at the end of which the invitation to X and Y had usually lapsed.

Her dominance on such occasions was remarkable. Her colleagues, particularly in her later years, were reduced to the condition of a group of schoolboys in the presence of an overbearing headmistress. Curiously, they seemed to adopt the manners appropriate to such a setting, heads down, exchanging furtive asides and jokes, and enjoying the discomfiture of a colleague who happened to engage the lady's alarming attentions.

There were exceptions. Nigel Lawson was intellectually confident and adopted a jaunty tone towards her, almost as a fellow conspirator. Norman Tebbit also stood out by the sharpness and independence of his views.

But the others were distinctly subdued. Douglas Hurd perhaps never overcame in her eyes his past as Heath's political secretary, which meant, I suppose, that he was regarded as, in the last analysis, ideologically unreliable. Whereas Geoffrey Howe, to pursue the educational image, was too often like the boy on the school playground who expects to be bullied and is for that very reason the magnet for the bully.

Her attitude to the Foreign Office was curious. For individual officials, who had shown themselves competent and who had helped her, she had much goodwill and would commend them, or ask for them to be consulted, years later. But mention of the Office in the collective sense brought out the worst in her. It was partly a reaction to the languid, superior manner, popularly associated with diplomats, which she may have encountered, or believed she had encountered, in her earlier forays as Leader of the Opposition. These were the 'laid-back generalists' of *The Downing Street Years*. It was partly that in a world less responsive to Britain's wishes than had once been the case, the diplomats, if they were doing their job properly, tended to carry unwelcome messages. 'It is not so straightforward as you think, Prime Minister.' 'If we act in such a way we must expect such and such a reaction.' In Norman Tebbit's caricature they became the ministry that looked after foreigners, in the same way that the Ministry of Agriculture looked after farmers. In her perpetual struggle against a hostile world she saw them as defeatists, even collaborators.

But in the end the problems lay deeper than that. Her increasing self-assertion in foreign affairs, her reliance on a small circle of advisers provoked counter-suspicions and resentments on the other side of Downing Street. It may have been a more balanced relationship in Lord Carrington's time as Foreign Secretary. But the seeds were probably already there.

> The young disease, that must subdue at length,
> Grows with his growth, and strengthens with his
> > strength.

By the second half of the 1980s no foreign affairs decision of any significance was made without reference to No. 10. The instinctive sympathy and understanding between Prime Minister and Foreign Secretary which lies at the heart of a successful foreign policy, and for which no well-meant interventions by advisers or officials can compensate, was lacking. The Foreign Secretary was too often thought of as not entirely reliable; and the fears became self-fulfilling. In a key area, Europe, two different policies emerged, and the contradictions exploded in Geoffrey Howe's resignation speech.

4

A View of the World

LOOKING BACK, I feel some surprise that Mrs Thatcher and I managed to get on so well for so many years. She was of course kind and tolerant, as with all her staff; but, these personal courtesies apart, there was a good working relationship, and when, after her re-election in 1987, I suggested she might want to make changes, she was quick to ask me to stay on.

In fact, on many fundamentals we were close. When I moved into No. 10 I wrote her a 'First Thoughts' paper, a kind of credo and a rough sketch of the international scene as I saw it. I began by saying that I took a bleak view of international affairs and, applying the words of the Athenian envoy in Thucydides, said it was still a world where the strong did what they could and the weak accepted what they must. (The reference earned me a wholly undeserved reputation with her as a classical scholar.) This was not to discount ideals, merely to note that there would be little chance of realizing them without military, political or, above all, economic strength.

I went on to say that I was profoundly pro-American. This was not a blank cheque for a chaotic administration and a violent and over-commercialized society. But it was a recognition that in the last analysis the United States spoke for freedom and provided the fundamental guarantee of our security. Over wide areas British and American policies naturally coincided. The tricky areas were where we differed. But British disagreement should always be tempered by the reflection that our capacity to influence events was limited and that the Americans held the preponderant power and responsibility.

The European Community would naturally be one of our major preoccupations; but, to put it as provocatively as possible, in terms of influence on the outside world the Community was for the future, the United States for the present.

I saw the Soviet Union as very much our principal external threat, not so much in the Third World, where Soviet advances were precarious, as in Western Europe. I did not see the chief danger as invasion, rather that the Soviet Union would extend and deepen its military shadow over Western Europe to the point where European policies were automatically modified to take account of Soviet wishes. To counter such a threat called for great firmness, resolution and persistence, particularly hard for a hetero-geneous collection of democracies with short memories, economic difficulties, and problems with public opinion naturally horrified at the potential of nuclear weapons. Businesslike dialogue with the Russians was essential, but we must cherish none of the illusions of *détente*.

Perhaps the West's greatest asset, certainly as seen from Communist countries, was its apparently effortless capacity to generate wealth and technological advance. A substantial Western economic recovery was therefore critical, politically as well as economically. Our advice to our partners and ourselves should be Guizot's '*Enrichissez-vous!*'

China, the other great Communist power, posed no threat to our interests, apart from Hong Kong. In fact, given the state of Sino-Soviet relations, China conferred great strategic benefits on the West, distracting the Soviet Union and tying down considerable Soviet forces.

And so on. It was necessarily generalized and now seems very dated. But it revealed much common ground, except perhaps on Europe, and on that foundation we were able to approach the detailed issues in an amicable and constructive way. A wary mutual respect was established. I was never in her innermost circle; my place was at one or two removes. But we could communicate easily and I could exercise influence in many areas I thought important.

There was another factor which made for co-operation. As de Gaulle with France, Mrs Thatcher had 'a certain idea' of Britain. She was concerned explicitly with its regeneration, both at home and abroad. This passionate commitment struck a chord with officials, including many who could not have been described as natural Thatcherites. Particularly in the diplomatic service. All of us who dealt with the outside world were acutely aware of the dwindling strength of Britain relative to her partners, the increasingly precarious economic base on which we were performing our political evolutions, making our *démarches*, conducting our negotiations, pushing for new markets. The 'question of Britain', the 'long decline', was present in all our minds. Sir Nicholas Henderson's leaked despatch from Paris was only the most celebrated example. And, as the United Kingdom slipped down the league-table, as the crises and IMF missions succeeded each other, we had sometimes a sense of performing in mid-air, Indian rope-trick fashion, without any base at all. For those who were inclined to forget it, the pitying or gleeful comments in the foreign press were insistent reminders of our fundamental problem.

Now the Prime Minister was tackling the disease and, it seemed, with some success. As she put it to an audience at Cheltenham in 1982, 'We have ceased to be a nation in retreat.' The economy was being transformed and the unions checked. The necessary gamble of the Falklands War had succeeded and the fact had been registered in chanceries and ministries of defence around the world. In her travels, and she travelled a great deal, the Prime Minister was tirelessly batting for Britain. If the tone was sometimes shrill and the vision over-simplified, no matter. We were on the move and, as we could all observe, being listened to once more.

In her later years as Prime Minister, particularly after the collapse of Soviet control in Eastern Europe, Mrs Thatcher was able to assume a wider role, as the prophet of political and economic freedom for other countries as well as Britain. This was at a time when reservations about pure Thatcherite doctrines were less common than today, when Britain was seen as the herald of democracy and prosperity abroad as well as a successful example of revival at home. Britain, it seemed, had the answers and British diplomacy was again at the cutting edge.

5

A Change of Regime

THIS THEN WAS the setting for foreign policy-making in the last seven years of Mrs Thatcher's premiership: a highly centralized administration, increasingly concentrated about one figure; a Prime Minister repeatedly re-elected, growing in authority and, as it seemed, in success; an atmosphere at No. 10 of hyperactivity and close loyalty; a view of the world that was simple, clear and dogmatic.

It was not a particularly altruistic view. There were ideals, the defence of Western ways of government and Western economic systems; a wish to ensure their spread if possible; a respect for international law; a commitment to international stability. These were seen as synonymous with the pursuit of British interests, and it was usually in terms of British interests, narrowly defined, that the governing analysis was made. In such papers there was more about British interests than common international interests. The United Nations was not forgotten but was seen more as a court where we must win our case than as a representative of some superior order. Aid was generously given, but with a wish to relate it more closely to British exports. And though the Prime Minister did not theorize on the subject, international society was seen less as a family of nations than in Hobbesian terms as a natural anarchy, where 'in all times kings and persons of sovereign authority, because of their independency are in continual jealousies and in the state and posture of gladiators'.

There was relatively little interplay between foreign and domestic policies, except in the case of Europe and, of course, Ireland. The assertion of British interests against foreigners, solidarity with the United States and NATO, strong defence, these represented natural constituencies. The quarrels with the Commonwealth over South Africa excited much media comment but probably had little impact on the general public.

It is often alleged that the government became too secretive and cynical and careless about its duties to Parliament. In fact the Prime Minister was punctilious about the rules; she would not have pleaded *raison d'état* in her defence. But foreign policy cannot be conducted in an atmosphere of moral outrage or under constant public scrutiny. It requires realism and confidentiality. We must deal with the world as we find it. A large proportion of the states we do business with are sadly deficient in human rights and democracy. But we cannot neglect them if we are to promote British interests; and our correspondence with them must be discreet if it is to be effective.

That said, it is true that the executive had acquired a great deal of power and was not much bothered by Parliament or the press. There was a solid majority in the Commons; the press was untroublesome. In any event, under the British system those conducting foreign policy were in the enviable position of being able to concentrate on their work, with little distraction from enquiring committees. Nor, in their infrequent encounters, were officials always impressed by the quality of their interrogators: the results tended to be like that in the post-Westlands meeting between Sir Robert Armstrong and the House of Commons Defence Committee, which the press summed up as 'Mandarins 3: MPs nil.' This state of affairs encouraged a certain detachment and even arrogance. Foreign policy approached what some would see as its ideal condition, a cool, technical exercise in pursuit of national interests, undisturbed by popular prejudice.

So all was well. But in the end there was trouble; and it arose largely from within, from the concentration of power, from the isolation it imposed, and from the character deformation it encouraged. We are all fated to become caricatures of ourselves. As time passed the lines were etched more deeply, the loyalties grew fiercer and more exclusive, the headquarters more embattled and bunker-like. Domestic policies were more violently controversial. After 1988 the economy was no longer a shining example. Events abroad also proved less responsive to the Prime Minister's formulae. The natural rapport with Washington of President Reagan's days was lost. And in one very important instance, that of German reunification, she was left Canute-like, shouting against the tide. There were many factors behind her fall; but Europe was certainly one.

The immediate reaction to her resignation among her staff was one of dismay and bewilderment. A central part of our world had disappeared. It was difficult to imagine life without her. But the mood was rapidly succeeded, and this applies probably more to ministers than officials, by a sense of relief. There was an almost audible sigh. The tension relaxed several notches; life became less heroic, less hazardous.

John Major's style was different. He was male, clubbable, standard-issue. He had a pleasant smile and listened to people. Ministers were surprised to be asked to express their opinion and to see it given weight. Habits of consensus returned. And the Cabinet Office hastened to restore the proper methods of doing business. In the necessary secrecy of the Gulf War Mrs Thatcher's highly personal habits of consulting and deciding had got near the point of disrupting the Whitehall machinery. The servicing of the War Cabinet was now taken over by the Cabinet Secretariat. No more records by the Private Secretary circulated to some but not to all. Charles Powell stayed on until the end of the war, in March 1991, and served the new Prime Minister loyally. He then retired to private business, to be succeeded by Stephen Wall, who took a more orthodox view of the Private Secretary's duties. I myself began to think of leaving and fixed a date a year ahead, by which time a suitable successor as Foreign Policy Adviser and Joint Intelligence Committee Chairman might be available.

It is not easy to characterize the setting in the first eighteen months of John Major's premiership. As in all beginnings, there were many legacies from the old regime. There was a war to conduct in concert with the United States and the coalition forged by President Bush and Secretary Baker. The lines were already laid down. After that there was the necessary surveillance of Iraq, again an inherited task.

But changes were being made. Domestic policies, particularly the Poll Tax, were being revised and softened. The attitude to Europe altered, from confrontation to negotiation. In a memorandum to the new Prime Minister reviewing the scene I did not say that Britain had to be at the heart of Europe. But I did say that our future lay in Europe and that we could not afford to be marginalized. I also reminded him that the overall success of our foreign policy depended crucially on two factors, our economic strength at home and the successful handling of our relations with the Community.

The international situation was also changing. The familiar landscape of the Cold War, with its solidarities and certainties, was breaking up and shifting into something like the present ambiguous scene. Of the two superpowers, the first, the United States, in theory dominant and triumphant, was in fact afflicted by a curious malaise, in part engendered by economic troubles, in part by a sense of what Professor Kennedy has called 'imperial overstretch'. The second, the Soviet Union, was no longer in the superpower category, but in a condition of disintegration and collapse.

There was now no single overwhelming threat to the West, but a series of lesser problems, not easily capable of analysis or resolution. The dissolution of the Soviet empire was releasing virulent old nationalist and ethnic antagonisms. It also threatened a dangerous dissemination of weapons technology. The great powers were growing more parochial, caught in economic recession and unwilling to undertake the commitments and face the losses in manpower needed to maintain international stability. The euphoria attending the end of the Gulf War, the hopes of a new international order, were proving short-lived. And the Gulf War itself was to prove a highly misleading precedent for post-Cold War crises, a war with the lightest of Western casualties, won by high-technology weapons, and financed largely by third parties.

To this equivocal scene the new Prime Minister brought no great shaping vision. In ideological terms he travelled light. He was quick, acute, mastered a brief rapidly and negotiated with skill. He was sensitive, if anything over-sensitive, to the domestic impact of his policies and the views of the media. He was responsive to advice. But his real views often remained elusive: he kept an open mind. He was above all a tactician and perhaps already had the sense that for him at that juncture of domestic politics the supreme virtue would be the ability to hold his party together.

With him orthodoxy returned to Whitehall business. There were more ministerial meetings, fewer private conclaves. Private secretaries kept their heads down. The Cabinet Secretariat serviced inter-departmental meetings as in the book; and I recall in particular widely attended ministerial meetings on Europe, based on standard Cabinet papers, an experience extremely rare in the preceding reign. There were fewer Chequers seminars, however, and fewer of Mrs Thatcher's attempts to raise eyes from immediate concerns and ask what the remoter prospects might be.

Here perhaps it is worth reminding readers of one factor affecting foreign policy which is only too familiar to the practitioner but which may be overlooked by the layman or the academic commentator. It operated equally under Margaret Thatcher and John Major and I am sure is as powerful today. I mean the almost unsustainable pressure of events and the blizzard of official paper which attempts to record and analyse them.

Ministers are governed by diaries which seem designed to break them in physique or spirit in the shortest possible time. There seems also a convention among private secretaries that gaps in the diary, spells that might be used for reflection or pure idleness, are in some fundamental way wicked, to be filled as soon as they threaten. Filling such gaps is in any case easy; and ministers themselves become part of the conspiracy, only too ready to retreat from thought into activity for activity's sake. Prime ministers are especially vulnerable. They face demands on their time from three main directions: from Parliament, with Prime Minister's Question Time twice a week and major debates on occasion; from the Party and the constituencies, culminating in extraordinary efforts at election times; and from the executive branch of government, for which foreign affairs is a major responsibility.

There is a prime ministerial round in international affairs, a kind of social season, a series of meetings at which, depending on the time of year, the best heads of government are to be found: the G7 gatherings of the leaders of the richest countries in the summer, the European summit meetings, and so on. In addition, there are official bilateral visits abroad and a steady stream of high-level visitors to be entertained in London.

This is the planned programme. But to it have to be added the unbudgeted requirements, what one historian has seen as the major element in history, 'the play of the contingent and the unforeseen':[3] the terrorist attack; the currency crisis; the new war in the Third World. There is never a shortage. In external relations governments commonly react to events rather than direct them.

This flux of happenings is recorded and analysed in piles of paper which modern communication skills make ever more threatening and unmanageable. I found I could spend the greater part of my day leafing through and reading the in and out telegrams delivered faithfully to my desk every few hours. Reading only, not taking action. For the Prime Minister there was a sifting process: only selected telegrams were submitted; but these were supplemented by comments and advice; and decisions had to be taken on them.

These pressures and the consequent culture of emergencies naturally affected thinking and behaviour and reduced the quality of response. Policy recommendations were made by overstretched advisers working at breakneck speed and digested by leaders under even greater stress. This meant a dependence on *idées reçues*, drafts on a dwindling intellectual capital amassed years before. It meant an even greater importance than usual given to day-to-day business. Attempts to plan ahead seemed unrealistic. The few meetings of this kind that survived were regularly hijacked by some new development; and ministers would turn with relief from the larger canvas to the familiar questions of the hour.

During my time with Mrs Thatcher I recall no meeting examining our long-term aims in Europe (though admittedly there were special factors at work here). And as the Balkan crisis developed in 1991, I found it impossible to get ministers to look at the likely outcome and to ask what we ourselves wanted and how best to attain it. This although we had been forecasting the violent disintegration of Yugoslavia since early 1990. Policy in these conditions was shaped less by longer-term aims than by a series of day-to-day decisions taken with little reference to a larger framework. The picture was built up in pointillist style by a series of small brush strokes. We felt our way forward and for too much of the time lived hand-to-mouth, locked in what Dr Kissinger has called the 'endless battle in which the urgent constantly gains on the important'.[4]

6

The Intelligence Dimension

I WAS ABLE TO watch foreign policy being made from my room at No. 10. I watched it also from another vantage point, a desk in the Cabinet Office, on the other side of that connecting door which *Yes, Prime Minister* has made so familiar. Here I was Chairman of the Joint Intelligence Committee (JIC) from 1985 to 1992. I had an office next to the Assessments Staff and the JIC Secretariat, with the duty intelligence officers keeping their unbroken watch from a room at the end of the corridor.

This was the hard world of shocks and accidents, threats and crises, the raw material of international life, before the policy-makers could impose their patterns on it. Here the news was usually bad, more about the errors, less about the achievements. It was the dark side of the moon, history pre-eminently as the record of the crimes and follies of mankind. The organization handling it was a central part of the Whitehall machinery, its work necessarily secret. But some account, however guarded, is required if I am to give an accurate picture of the course of government and policy in those years.

The Joint Intelligence Committee was set up in 1936 by that great administrative architect, Sir Maurice Hankey, as a sub-committee of the Chiefs of Staff. Its aim from the outset was to unify, to draw together the disparate pieces of intelligence coming into British hands and to present them as a coherent judgement on which the decision-makers, seen at that time as mainly military, could build. At first, however, it was a very subordinate body and lumbered with too many tasks; the Chiefs received it only occasionally; and its unity was no more than nominal: it was dominated by armed service rivalries, each branch of military intelligence guarding its own assets and point of view.

The Second World War and the influence of Churchill, who devoured intelligence and hankered after a unified intelligence service, gave the Committee new authority. It began to meet weekly with the Chiefs and it was given a Joint Intelligence Staff (JIS) to draft its papers. Churchill made it a crisis organization, directing it 'to take the initiative in preparing at any hour of the day or night as a matter of urgency papers on any particular development'. It acquired an astute Foreign Office chairman, Bill Cavendish-Bentinck, who, as Noel Annan tells us in his absorbing account of the wartime JIC, managed the admirals and generals with skill and was not afraid to back his own judgement.[5] And though JIC forecasts, as always, were fallible, the immense operational successes of British intelligence during the war, whether Ultra or Double Cross, brought reflected glory to the analytical part of the machine.

After the war, despite the existence of the JIS and the aspiration towards a unified assessment service, the problem for the analysts remained a lack of sufficient weight and authority at the centre to offset the power of individual Whitehall departments. In 1957 the JIC moved to the Cabinet Office, reflecting the widening scope of its work. But it was not until the reforms of 1968, guided by Sir Burke Trend, Sir Dick White and Sir Denis Greenhill, that a sufficiently strong unit was established there to ensure a view of events which would prevail against departmental interpretations.

It was this quintessential mandarin trio who can claim the credit for the modern Joint Intelligence Organization. The key reform was the creation of the Assessments Staff, a group of between twenty and thirty officials and service officers, seconded to the Cabinet Office to chair the JIC's subcommittees (the Current Intelligence Groups) and to prepare assessments on an interdepartmental basis.

One further change occurred after the Falklands War, again in the direction of greater freedom from departmental influence. The Franks Report recommended that the Chairman of the JIC should be given a more critical and independent role and as a result the post passed to the Cabinet Office from the Foreign Office, where it had been held since the days of Cavendish-Bentinck. The Chairman was now appointed by the Prime Minister and had direct access to her.

The machine I inherited had therefore gained greatly in independence and authority over the years. It no longer reported to the Chiefs of Staff, but directly to the Prime Minister and a small number of his senior colleagues. Its assessments covered political and economic as well as military developments and were so prepared that they represented the collective expertise of Whitehall on a particular issue, drawing on all relevant departments and all relevant information, from a news report at one end of the spectrum to the most highly classified piece of intelligence at the other. As a result, a contributing department could not later dissent from the collective judgement and ministers were given a solid foundation of assessment and prediction on which to base policy. The Weekly Digest of Intelligence, the Red Book, waiting on the Prime Minister's desk every Friday morning, gave a brief conspectus of situations abroad likely to impinge on British interests, and of the Irish terrorist threat, so that he and his colleagues would not be too surprised by events and might even be able to anticipate some.

If, as often happened, events were moving faster, the weekly survey would be supplemented by Immediate Assessments issued at short notice. In times of high crisis the machine moved up a further gear. During the Gulf War, the Middle East Current Intelligence Group would meet through the night to ensure that the War Cabinet had an up-to-date judgement before it at its daily morning meeting.

In addition to the papers recording these collective judgements, there was a constant traffic between the Cabinet Office and No. 10, as the Chairman of the JIC drew individual intelligence reports to the attention of the Prime Minister, with comments on their significance. In his other capacity he would also write a minute on the weekly Red Book, drawing attention to the most important items and their policy implications.

In normal times the Committee met every Thursday morning at the same time as the Cabinet. The heads of the intelligence agencies, the Head of the Security Service, the Head of the Secret Intelligence Service (SIS) and the Director of GCHQ were ex-officio members. In addition there were the Chief of Defence Intelligence, senior officials from the Foreign Office, the Ministry of Defence and the Treasury, plus the Intelligence Co-ordinator, who saw to the smooth running of the machine, supervised the finances and helped lay down its priorities. Finally, the Head of the Assessments Staff, presenting the week's assessments.

This was the high table of intelligence. Beneath it were the individual intelligence agencies, the collectors, whose raw intelligence, circulating to interested Whitehall departments, provided the grist for the analysts' mill. There was the JIC Secretariat and there was the small corps of analysts, the Assessments Staff, organized in Current Intelligence Groups on a part-geographical, part-functional basis.

It was a formidable machine, perhaps overweight for Britain in its reduced modern condition, but a powerful asset to be exploited to the full. I was always impressed by the skill and wisdom of its members and felt it a privilege to work with them.

We provided a world-wide coverage, corresponding to the world-wide spread of British interests. The staples were East-West relations, the Middle and Far East, terrorism in all its guises, the spread of weapons of mass destruction, South Africa. Economic issues like oil prices were included. The international drugs trade was a new topic, the threat to the Falklands an old one, regularly revisited. But trouble, or the prospect of trouble, from China to Peru, provided it had implications for Britain, demanded and received its mention and its judgement. And though economies often meant the closure of embassies and stations, and should in theory have removed the obligation to report, ministers still expected the old, all-inclusive, wall-to-wall service.

The organization had strong American links, reflecting a common world outlook and dating back to the wartime alliance. The greater part of the output was pooled and, given the scale of US resources, we drew from it much more than we put in. But in certain areas we provided an irreplaceable contribution and in general the Americans sought a second opinion from another world-wide operator whose skill and discretion could be relied on.

It was no longer a sentimental partnership, if it ever had been, rather a businesslike arrangement, from which both sides profited greatly. In Washington they ran a different system, based on the *laissez-faire* principle that truth emerges from contending agencies and interpretations, and they thought sometimes that our judgements were too varnished, with not enough dissenting opinion. But they admired their quality and sometimes passed them up to the President. The fact that the two governments were working from a common data base had in itself large implications.

We were in constant contact at all levels. I used to pay regular visits to Washington to talk with the head of the CIA and the National Security Adviser in the White House about the state of the world; and on such trips I felt less than at any other time that sense of inequality that customarily descends on British government representatives in those parts.

Much of the JIC's work was concerned with reporting and interpreting on-going action, such as the Iran-Iraq War, or troop movements on the Sino-Soviet frontier, and ensuring that the factual base on which policy decisions were taken was as thorough and accurate as possible. But there was another dimension. The Committee was charged with monitoring and giving 'early warning of the development of direct or indirect foreign threats to British interests whether political, military or economic'. Here we stepped on to much less solid ground and became one of the main pieces of government machinery tasked to predict the future. Apart from the Meteorological Office, the Treasury economic forecasters were perhaps our only rivals. We never compared notes; but I like to think we performed rather better.

It was, of course, an impossible task, though it is remarkable that the failure rate was kept so low. Intelligence successes are unsung. They are usually the things that do not happen: the terrorist attempt that fails; the piece of international negotiation smoothly concluded; the thoughts of aggression that become second thoughts. What was accomplished would be revealed, if at all, after the passage of years, like the greater achievements of our predecessors in the Second World War. The inevitable failures, on the other hand, were given instant fame.

It was a curious assignment. To assist us we had great technical resources, overhead satellites, decoding machines. We were the heirs of Enigma. But at the same time we were members of an older and shadier fraternity, all those who over the centuries have claimed to read the future for their masters: the shamans and soothsayers, sybils and readers of entrails, Macaulay's 'pale augurs muttering low'. I had often in my mind the message on one of the oracle-bones in an ancient Chinese capital I had visited: 'Will there be a disaster in the next weeks?' It was in effect the question the JIC had to ask itself every day of its existence.

The art of predictive assessment, for it could claim to be an art or craft, lay in interpreting fragmentary and usually ambiguous intelligence and constructing on that basis a picture of the other side's plans. Analysis was a misleading term in that context: the work was imaginative and creative. The key lay in the ability to enter the mind of the foreign leader in question. Capabilities could be measured, the number of tanks or aircraft, and their location pin-pointed; but intentions were almost always a mystery. There was a natural tendency to ascribe rationality to the other side and to assume your man would act in accordance with his best interests as a reasonable person in possession of all the facts would calculate them. Rationality was, after all, the condition of intelligent discourse; without it the world was entirely arbitrary and unfathomable. The trouble was that most of our clients, from Kim Il Sung to Saddam Hussein, were both powerful and irrational. Their minds did not necessarily operate according to our calculus.

There were other hazards. There was a natural inclination, having formed a view of the other side's strategy, to stick to it and downgrade conflicting indicators. So, during the Second World War, reports of German armour in the area were discounted before Arnhem. So Stalin suspected and dismissed intelligence of impending German invasion. And the Americans before Pearl Harbor, though aware that the Japanese were about to break off negotiations, were still influenced by old convictions that an attack would be towards South-east Asia and the East Indies. One becomes very attached to one's views and the mind has excellent mechanisms for excluding discordant facts.

There was also the temptation to play safe and cry 'Wolf!' every time. No analyst has lost his post by predicting disaster: he invariably escapes in the relief felt when lightning does not strike. But he has devalued the currency. The brave prediction, though also the most hazardous, is that there will not be war.

The great prize was to read intentions. But at one level, that of defence planning, it was capabilities that mattered and worst-case scenarios that had to be employed. Gorbachev's reforms in the Soviet Union gave grounds for hope and the new possibilities were reflected in assessments. But while Soviet divisions and missiles remained in place in Eastern Europe the military assumption had to be that they could be used and the necessary dispositions had to be made. On a balance of probability we could expect, and predict, better days; but in the area of defence no responsible military or political leader can afford to take chances. There is always a substratum of caution, even pessimism, in intelligence communities, arising from their warning role, their greater awareness of the dangers and their intimate connection with national security.

The combination of the posts of Foreign Policy Adviser and JIC Chairman was a great help to me at No. 10. It gave me a supporting staff of a kind that the Downing Street arrangements denied; and it gave greater weight to my recommendations. But it was unorthodox, and reservations were expressed, as I recall, by the Foreign Secretary and the Secretary to the Cabinet. They were briskly overruled by the Prime Minister. But they had some foundation in normal practice. Intelligence and policy are usually kept apart in separate rooms. The partition has to be thin, otherwise assessments, however interesting to their composers, fail to answer the questions uppermost in ministers' minds. But if there is no partition, there is a risk of intelligence being slanted to provide the answers the policy-makers want. This is a grave sin: the analyst must convey his message, usually unpalatable, without fear or favour. And we thought we saw signs of this policy-led distortion in CIA estimates on Central America when Bill Casey was Director and the Contra operation was in full flow. So much so that we felt obliged to build our own sources.

In theory the danger was present in my case. In practice it did not arise. I felt no temptation to cook the books; and if I had, my JIC colleagues would not have tolerated it. As it was, my advice gained in weight; and I enjoyed an extra means of access to the study at No. 10.

Mrs Thatcher respected intelligence and had a keen appetite for it. She was aware from personal experience that we lived in a dangerous world. She was a realist and recognized that we were not likely to learn the true intentions of foreign governments, let alone terrorist groups, from the public prints or even the diplomatic telegrams. I suspect she also experienced, as many ministers do, a certain frisson at the receipt of those heavily classified pieces of paper, with their air of urgency and menace, and their flattering suggestion of superior and exclusive knowledge. She was aware that Britain had a powerful intelligence machine, was good at the game, and enjoyed in consequence valuable influence in Washington. That mattered. Certainly, I always found her receptive and supportive. This extended to funding, always a difficult issue, as technical intelligence grew ever more expensive. She accepted the estimates promptly, scarcely giving the Chancellor time to comment. In Nigel Lawson's memoirs there are some sour observations reflecting this experience.

She was scrupulous about security. The strictly personal message would come back in a double envelope addressed in her own hand. She would not comment publicly on intelligence. She had made two unusually full statements, on Anthony Blunt and Sir Roger Hollis, in 1979 and 1981, before my time. But while I was there the invariable answer to questions was, 'It is not customary to comment on intelligence matters.'

I wanted her to be a little more forthcoming, since total silence left the field open to the self-proclaimed experts, the fantasists and the ill-disposed, who were always busy. I would have liked the occasional public reminder that the intelligence community was serving the nation's interests well in a violent world, ensuring that we could sleep safely in our beds and alerting us to the activities of our enemies abroad; and that official silence denoted only the necessary convention of secrecy, not, as popularly supposed, incompetence or inability to answer the media travesties. But she would not be drawn. This same determination to apply the rules lay behind the controversial decision to pursue Peter Wright through the Australian courts.

She saw little reason to change the rules on accountability for intelligence. The Foreign Secretary answered in Parliament for the Secret Intelligence Service and GCHQ, the Home Secretary for the Security Service. She herself had overall responsibility. She approved action to put the Security Service on a statutory footing with the Security Service Act of 1989. But she was not in favour of a parliamentary oversight committee.

This change came with her successor. I was not at first in favour of it, but accept that in its present form it may give public reassurance that the intelligence services are working as they should be. Nevertheless, the idea of openly accountable services remains a contradiction in terms. To be of any value, the work must be done, and defended, in secret. It may assist public confidence if responsible outsiders are indoctrinated and introduced behind the curtain. But they must remain there, bound by the same rules of silence. The reassurance can come only from the public knowledge that they are there and are not outraged by what they see. It is also important that the overseers should not be so exhaustive or hostile in their enquiries that the energies of the services are diverted from their proper task of gathering and analysing intelligence to that of self-justification.

During those eight years, intelligence and policy were as closely linked as they have ever been in British government. The value and prestige of the intelligence services gained in consequence. How was policy affected? The policy-makers were well informed and often forearmed. British ministers had consistently better briefs than foreign colleagues. The Prime Minister was given the under-pinning for a robust and expert response to the multifarious threats to British interests, from Soviet missiles to terrorist plots. It might be argued that she was thereby confirmed in her tendency to see the world in black and white. I would not agree: she began with few illusions; and a significant part of the information, as over the effect of Gorbachev's reforms in Eastern Europe and the Soviet Union itself, was of a world moving along more hopeful lines. One effect of possibly greater weight was that the close American link emphasized the Atlanticist bias in her policy and may have encour-aged the belief that for Britain close ties to the United States could suffice.

*   *   *

As an historical footnote, I should record that the organizational arrangements I have described above did not long survive the transition from Margaret Thatcher to John Major. The setting changed. When I retired, in June 1992, I was able to pass the com-bined package of responsibilities, Foreign Policy Adviser cum JIC Chairman, to my successor, Sir Rodric Braithwaite, formerly Ambassador in Moscow. It was a solid inheritance. But Rodric decided on retirement after eighteen months only, in January 1994. After him the post of Foreign Policy Adviser lapsed. There had been only three incumbents.

An Assistant Private Secretary was added on the foreign affairs side in No. 10 in compensation. In the Cabinet Office, the post of Chairman of the JIC was given to the Deputy Secretary in the Cabinet Secretariat, relatively junior, on secondment from the Foreign Office, and with considerable duties under Sir Robin Butler of a non-intelligence kind.

So a great fief was divided and, like barons recovering their lands on the removal of some medieval king's favourite, the Foreign Secretary and Cabinet Secretary reasserted their traditional positions. It was inevitable and perhaps appropriate: the No. 10 staffing arrangements had reflected a special period in British government. Whether they should be revived under a future Prime Minister is a subject that deserves careful thought and planning. But I suspect it will be decided in the usual *ad hoc* fashion.

Part II

Policies

7

The United States:
A Very, Very Special Relationship

SOLIDARITY WITH THE United States as a cardinal principle of foreign policy acquired a special sanctity under Margaret Thatcher; but as a working rule it had been in place for many British governments over many years. Professor Kennedy has noted a long series of British acts of deference to the Americans, going back at least as far as the *Alabama* settlement of 1872 and continuing with the Anglo-American Naval Agreement of 1921, 'a steady tilting of the scales from the older, declining power to the newer, expanding one'.[6]

After the Second World War, when the scales had tilted very much further, US-UK solidarity reflected the hard realities of relative power, the fact of American military and economic dominance, and European reliance on the United States as the ultimate guarantor of Western freedom in the face of the threat from the Soviet Union. In the narrower bilateral context, British security was even more closely tied to that of America: the 1962 Polaris deal, concluded between Macmillan and President Kennedy, confirmed British dependence on the United States for the British nuclear deterrent.

Wartime comradeship, a common language and memories of a common achievement cushioned these unpalatable facts. The habits of consultation and collaboration established under

Roosevelt and Churchill survived and flourished in the peace and laid the foundation for what was called, with varying degrees of truth, depending on the time and the issue involved, the special relationship.

Individual prime ministers were more or less pro-American, Heath least so, Churchill and Macmillan devotees. But for all, over very wide areas, British and US interests were close if not identical; and where they were not, British governments of whatever political complexion had to think long and hard before openly diverging.

Looking at the scene in early 1984, I saw it in terms of two great tectonic plates, which for most of their surface overlapped and were as one; but the congruence was not perfect, leaving certain projecting areas; and it was on those rough edges that misunderstanding and friction could most readily arise. We saw most nearly eye-to-eye on the central questions of security and relations with the Soviet Union: the Middle East, Central America and the Caribbean, Ireland and, of course, trade issues were among the potential troublespots.

The disparity in strength meant that the relationship was always more important for the British than the American partner. The United States had to a much greater degree the power of major independent action; Britain's limitations in this respect had been cruelly brought home at the time of Suez. Britain acted upon the world directly, but also, and sometimes in a more effective way, at second hand, through Washington. And British capacity to influence international events was naturally at its highest when this second channel was operating most smoothly and the Administration and, above all, the President were most receptive to our analyses and prescriptions. Close British association had its benefits for the Americans, who generally did not wish to act in isolation. But it had much greater benefits for London: it gave an extra dimension to British foreign policy, a further lease of life to British influence across the board.

Close study of American intentions and easy access to Washington decision-makers were therefore primary requirements for the Foreign Office. The immediate response in any crisis was to ask what was the US reaction. Consultation with European part- ners grew, but was a secondary priority. The disorderly nature of policy-making in Washington, with noisy semi-public arguments among agencies and with Congress, made British intervention in some ways easier, but often left ultimate US decisions obscure and unpredictable. Yet it was essential to know what these would be: America had the capacity to change the international weather and present Britain with a new climate, which could involve painful choices between our narrower interests and the demands of solidarity.

Much thought was naturally devoted to these prospects; and it was not the easiest of tasks. When their interests were directly con- cerned, particularly at close hand, as in the Caribbean, the Americans could act fast and ruthlessly. There was often little warning, except that over the normal sunny surface of the consultation process a fog would descend. With a proactive Administration like that of President Reagan the need for foresight was even greater.

For Mrs Thatcher there were powerful factors underlining the importance of US-UK links. Studying the Suez débâcle, she had, as she tells us in her memoirs, drawn from it certain lessons, among them the maxim: 'We must never again find ourselves on the oppo- site side to the United States in a major international crisis affecting Britain's interests.'[7]

This was the warning of history. Publicly, she preferred to put the message in a more positive way. On her visit to Washington in 1981 she spoke of a new transatlantic partnership aimed at pro- moting stability, preventing aggression and opposing tyranny. The message, she said, was that 'we in Britain stand with you . . . Your problems will be our problems and when you look for friends we will be there.'

Again, in Washington in 1985 she said: 'We see so many things in the same way and you can speak of a real meeting of minds. I feel no inhibitions about describing the relationship as very, very special.'[8]

Also on the positive side was her intimacy with President

Reagan. In some ways this was an unlikely partnership: the bossy, intrusive Englishwoman, lecturing and hectoring, hyperactive, obsessively concerned with detail, an ex-chemist and lawyer, thin on imagination, strong on analysis; and the lazy, sunny, Irish ex-actor, his mind operating mostly in the instinctive mode, happy to delegate or over-delegate, hazy about most of his briefs, but with certain stubbornly held principles, a natural warmth and an extraordinary ability to communicate with his constituents.

But the two had a shared faith: a belief in the power of free enterprise and the need to spread the message of the market; and a passionate opposition to Communism. Neither was afraid of action. They also liked each other and, out of instinct or policy, became close friends. The President was courtly with the ladies and, it has been suggested, had a soft spot for dominant women. Certainly he admired Mrs Thatcher's harangues even when they were directed at him. He saw in her an invaluable ideological ally against the Washington establishment.

For her part, the Prime Minister when dealing with him exercised charm and tact in unusual measure. She had no illusions about her friend's intellectual capacities, but she was well aware of the power of his office and the strength of his personal beliefs. After a while she gave up lecturing him on the need to balance his budget; and she soon came to realize that his attachment to the Strategic Defense Initiative made it, whatever its objective merits, a fact on the international scene which could not be erased and had better be embraced.

They had got on well from their first meeting, in London in 1975, when neither was yet in office and Mrs Thatcher had, fortunately, given her guest more time than he received from the junior Labour minister who was his only government contact. Once they were in power they co-operated naturally.

The Administration was regularly generous in meeting British defence needs. An early problem arose over the replacement of Trident missiles. As recently as July 1980 Mrs Thatcher had exchanged letters with President Carter agreeing to buy Trident C-4 missiles to take the place of the obsolescent Polaris missiles acquired by Macmillan in the early 1960s. But very early in his first term Reagan decided to replace the C-4s with the larger, more accurate Trident D-5. This presented the British with an awkward and expensive renegotiation if they were to avoid once again being left with outdated equipment. But the American team were flexible and helpful, on presidential instruction, and the new missiles were secured on favourable terms – terms which, according to John Nott, the Defence Secretary at the time, were even more advantageous than in the case of the earlier deal with President Carter.

There was more striking support during the Falklands War. American practical assistance for the British forces was quiet, rapid and on a very wide scale. It was probably decisive in the recapture of the islands. It ranged from the use of the US base on Ascension Island to the supply of Sidewinder air-to-air missiles, Stinger anti-aircraft systems, aviation fuel, weapons and ammunition of all kinds, and even to the offer of a US aircraft-carrier. This supply began as soon as the British task force was embarked and ran on even during the confusing period of Secretary Haig's attempted mediation. The moving spirit here was Caspar Weinberger, the US Defense Secretary, but he could not have acted without Reagan's general approval.

At the same time the President made occasional interventions of a more ambivalent kind, as when he telephoned the Prime Minister in May after British troops had secured a landing on the Falklands to point out the ill effects in Latin America and elsewhere of too overwhelming a British victory and to suggest that Britain might now gracefully withdraw, leaving some international umbrella organization to take over the administration of the islands. He received a blistering refusal.

These passages apart, Trident and the Falklands were big entries on the credit side of the relationship. But Anglo-American diplomacy is delicate and exacting at the best of times, and in those first four years of the Reagan presidency there were two major incidents that illustrated how easily the partners could fall out. They concerned trade and the Caribbean, two natural troublespots in this context.

The first, coinciding with the Falklands War, flowed from the imposition of martial law in Poland in 1981. In response, the NATO allies had agreed to undertake certain modest sanctions directed against both the Polish and the Soviet governments. The US Administration went further and announced measures including a ban on licences for the sale of oil and gas equipment to the Soviet Union. The real target of these extra sanctions was the pipeline supplying natural gas from Siberia to West Germany on which Chancellor Schmidt had agreed with Brezhnev as recently as November 1981. The Americans had opposed the deal, fearing it would make West Germany dangerously dependent on the Russians for their energy supplies. They found in the Polish crisis a convenient pretext for sabotaging an agreement they did not like. Their action was at first confined to US companies, but in June 1982 it was extended, with little thought for the consequences, to US subsidiaries and foreign companies as well.

The Prime Minister took strong exception to this last move, both on grounds of principle, as an attempt to assert extraterritorial jurisdiction, and more particularly because a Scottish company had large contracts for the pipeline. She visited Washington and made her views plain to the President's advisers; tactfully, she avoided direct confrontation with the President himself. In the House of Commons in July 1982 she condemned the attempt by 'one very powerful nation' to prevent the fulfilment of existing contracts; and the government used special powers to prevent British companies from complying with US orders. She improved the occasion by later saying, 'I feel I have been particularly wounded by a friend.' The independence and frankness of these comments were remarkable, given their timing (the end of the Falklands War) and British indebtedness to Washington in that conflict.

In the end, in November 1982, after much persuasion by George Shultz, Haig's successor as Secretary of State, the President announced he was lifting sanctions in return for agreement within NATO to a more restrictive approach to economic dealings with the Soviet Union.

He was later helpful in another dispute over extraterritorial powers, the legal action in the United States by the creditors of Laker Airways against British Airways, which in turn threatened British Airways' privatization. Both criminal and civil actions were eventually called off, after constant pressure by the Prime Minister.

The second, and sharper, crisis came later in the President's first term with the US invasion of Grenada in October 1983. This was the first of those unilateral US actions which, actual or prospective, so preoccupied No. 10 and the Foreign Office in the next few years. It was, by the standards of such operations, successful: it removed a bloodthirsty, extreme-left junta from an island uncomfortably close to the United States; it involved little bloodshed; and American forces rapidly extricated themselves. But it aroused, and rightly so, strong criticism and opposition on the British side.

There was first the question of consultation. Repeated inquiries in Washington in the days before the invasion had been met by repeated assurances that we would be consulted before any US action was taken. In fact the Prime Minister was informed by the President when his mind was made up and only hours before US troops went in. On the strength of Washington's assurances the Foreign Secretary, answering questions in the House on the afternoon of 24 October, again only hours before the attack, had emphasized that we were in close touch with the US authorities and had dismissed military intervention as unlikely. We had been made to look silly and the value of the US connection greatly degraded.

Then there was the fear that a precedent was being set. If the US Administration was to prove so trigger-happy and secretive, we could be faced at short notice with similar adventures in the future, posing the dilemma of publicly dissenting from our chief ally, or supporting an operation we ourselves judged unwise, or even wrong.

There was also an embarrassing aspect: Grenada was an independent Commonwealth country with a Governor-General in residence. The Queen's representative, the only constitutional authority on the island, was treated with scant respect. There was strong Commonwealth criticism.

But the aspect that most worried the Prime Minister was that of international law and the parallel with the Soviet invasion of Afghanistan in 1979. How to distinguish the two cases? Speaking on the BBC World Service on 30 October, she said, 'We in the Western countries, the Western democracies, use our force to defend our way of life. We do not use it to walk into independent sovereign territories . . . If you are going to pronounce a new law that wherever Communism reigns against the will of the people, even though it's happened internally, there the USA shall enter, then we are going to have really terrible wars in the world.'

Grenada blew over. The British government avoided official condemnation, in Parliament or the Security Council. Reagan was disappointed and puzzled but bore no ill will. The successful intervention helped in his re-election. Mrs Thatcher remained worried, however. I encountered echoes of the episode when I moved into No. 10. We had a seminar on a related theme at Chequers in the autumn and I recall writing a paper for her entitled 'Justified Invasions'.

8

The United States:
The Strategic Defense Initiative

GRENADA RAISED IMPORTANT points of principle but, strictly considered, was an incident on the fringe. The core of the US-UK dialogue, as always, concerned security, both Britain's defences and the common Western defences against the Soviet Union. This was in large part the province of the NATO alliance, the issues of conventional forces and intermediate-range and short-range missiles in Europe, and the balance between defence on the one hand and *détente* on the other. Here Britain naturally played a major role as a leading member of the alliance and one which, particularly in Mrs Thatcher's time, took up a position close to that of the United States.

But dialogue also extended to the strategic balance between the superpowers, the negotiations on strategic arms (START) and the recurrent attempts to control the alarming increase in number and sophistication of land- and sea-based intercontinental ballistic missiles. Here Britain had a lesser voice: the missiles were almost all in the hands of the United States and the Soviet Union; and a large part of the British concern was to ensure that the small British deterrent was not drawn too early into the grand equation and that its effectiveness was not reduced in other ways. Nevertheless, Britain had a nuclear responsibility and excellent intelligence and could provide a good second opinion. At times of high British influence in Washington British views could be significant in this field also. The Prime Minister had clear opinions on all these matters and was not at all hesitant in expressing them.

The centre of attention in President Reagan's first term had been in Europe and related to the threat posed by Soviet SS20 missiles. These were powerful new land-based intermediate-range weapons, deployed in steadily growing numbers since 1977 and capable of reaching anywhere in Europe from bases in the Soviet Union or, for that matter, a range of targets in China, Japan and South Korea from bases in Soviet Asia. The SS20 was mobile and therefore had survival capacity; it also had three independently targetable nuclear warheads. It represented a qualitative advance in weaponry and to Western governments was a very worrying development.

There was no American equivalent and the Soviet object was clearly to intimidate Western Europe and eventually decouple it from America by threatening the possibility of attack in circumstances in which the United States could not be relied upon to take part. A readiness to sacrifice Chicago for Hamburg seemed doubtful, if not implausible.

To meet the threat of blackmail posed by the SS20s NATO governments had accepted the deployment in their countries of US Cruise and Pershing II missiles and these deployments were beginning in late 1983. European peace movements, much encouraged by Soviet propaganda, put up a vociferous opposition. The American government endeavoured to negotiate the lowest possible level of medium-range missiles for both sides, ideally their elimination, and offered to cancel deployment of Cruise or Pershing if the Russians would agree to dismantle their equivalents.

The Russians for their part sought to formalize their advantage by calling for a nuclear freeze and, on the day the first Pershing II missiles arrived in Germany, walked out of the negotiations, promising never to return while deployments continued.

The Prime Minister was at home in this direct trial of wills. She was at one with Washington in insisting that the deployment of Cruise and Pershing should go forward at the same time as offers were made of negotiation to reduce the number of missiles on each side (the Dual Track). She was less happy with the proposal to remove American and Soviet missiles altogether: she thought this unreal and was alive to the value of US intermediate-range missiles in strengthening the strategic link between Europe and the States. She readily accepted the deployment of Cruise in Britain; and she did all she could to stiffen the less resolute members of the alliance.

When I became involved in discussion of these issues the Cruise missiles were arriving at Greenham Common and the fight for public opinion was in full swing. But the key NATO decisions had already been taken; the alliance stood firm. Eventually, a year later, the Russians climbed down and returned to the negotiating table; and the first steps were taken towards what was to be the Intermediate-Range Missile Treaty of 1987. In retrospect the episode stands out as a critical victory for the West.

From 1984 onwards, however, the emphasis of the US-UK dialogue on security shifted from Europe to the question of strategic weapons. Here discussion became dominated and, as some maintained at the time, distorted, by an extraordinary new concept, the Strategic Defense Initiative (SDI), popularly known as Star Wars. This was the President's personal contribution to the strategic debate. It reflected some of his most deeply held beliefs. It was controversial, depending on frontier science and turning traditional security logic upside down. It aroused deep suspicion and fear on the part of the Soviet Union and only slightly less apprehension on the part of some of America's allies. As we can now see, it probably played a significant part in the Soviet Union's defeat in the Cold War. It also, more by luck than good management, saved the United States and the West from a disastrous security setback at Reykjavik in 1986.

For many years peace between the United States and the Soviet Union had rested on a balance of terror. Each side had enough nuclear missiles to survive a first strike by the other and to retaliate by inflicting unacceptable damage. This shared knowledge was the effective deterrent against war. Arrayed in theoretical terms it became the doctrine of Mutually Assured Destruction (MAD). It was deterrence based on the reign of offensive weapons. As soon as the two superpowers met to discuss and regulate the strategic balance, anti-ballistic missile defences were confined, under the Anti-Ballistic Missile Treaty (ABM) of 1972 and the protocol of 1974, to one site per country. The Americans later decided to forego even this one site; the Russians showed more interest and maintained and upgraded a defensive system round Moscow.

President Reagan thought, or felt, along different lines. He recoiled from the idea of mutual destruction and reliance on it as the only means of deterring war. He was unwilling to accept that the United States should have no defence against missile attack, that the fundamental relationship with the Soviet Union had to be, in Oppenheimer's image, that of two scorpions in a bottle.

In a speech on 23 March 1983, after only partial consultation with his senior advisers, he offered a different basis for security, one that did not rely solely on offensive retaliation. Would it not be better, he asked, to embark on a programme to counter the Soviet missile threat with defensive systems which could intercept and destroy strategic ballistic missiles before they reached US soil, or that of America's allies? This would be a daunting technical task, requiring years, or even decades, of effort; and during that time the United States would have to be constant in preserving the nuclear deterrent and ensuring the security of its allies. But it was a task within the scope of American abilities and it was right to try.

> I call upon the scientific community in our country, those who gave us nuclear weapons, to turn their great talents now to the cause of mankind and world peace, to give us the means of rendering these nuclear weapons impotent and obsolete.
>
> Tonight . . . I am directing a comprehensive and inclusive effort to define a long-term research and development program to begin to achieve our ultimate goal of eliminating the threat posed by strategic nuclear missiles.

This was visionary and heretical; and it received a very sceptical press. But the ideas behind it had germinated long before, when the President was still Governor of California and a Republican candidate, making his first visits to defence headquarters and learning of their vulnerability to nuclear blast; and he clung stubbornly to them. They embraced rather more than a search for defensive technology. Alongside that ran another strand of thought, frequently touched on by him, but perhaps not given enough weight by those whose business it was to study US policies, namely a strong revulsion against nuclear weapons of all kinds and a desire eventually to get rid of them altogether. This anti-nuclear aspiration was to have profound consequences for his later discussions with Mikhail Gorbachev.

In her memoirs Lady Thatcher leaves the impression that she embraced the Strategic Defense Initiative rapidly, instinctively and with few reservations; that as a scientist she was in her element when dealing with it; and that doubts were confined to what she calls 'the laid-back generalists' of the Foreign Office, not to mention 'the ministerial muddlers in charge of them'. As I recall, it was rather more complicated than that. SDI, as at first outlined, gave considerable grounds for concern among America's allies, which the Prime Minister shared. There is also good evidence that in the early days she expressed these anxieties to the US Administration. It is worth recalling what some of our worries were.

There was first uncertainty about the technology. Would it, even within the long period envisaged by the President, be able to provide a reliable defence, and at a tolerable cost? If such a defence were achieved for America, what would be the position of Western Europe? Would it not mean Fortress America, with a dangerously insecure Europe outside the ramparts?

If ballistic missiles were rendered ineffective, what happened to Cruise missiles and bombers, the so-called 'air-breathing systems'? What would happen to the ABM Treaty as research proceeded? And as research passed into development and testing? What did the treaty permit?

Would not the shift from an offensive to a defensive strategy prove profoundly destabilizing? Crude though the concept was, the knowledge of mutually assured destruction had kept the peace for several decades. Would not the new philosophy lead to the deployment of even more offensive missiles with the object of saturating and overwhelming the opposing defences? As one side approached an adequate defence while retaining offensive missiles, would it not then be in a position to launch a safe first strike? And would not the other side, seeing the growing danger, be tempted to attack first before the screen became impenetrable?

Above all, would not the Soviet Union, already engaged in upgrading its missile defences, match US development with redoubled efforts? The result would be to degrade the British, and French, deterrents.

These and similar questions were in all our minds and those of our European allies. The Prime Minister was certainly alive to them. What distinguished her attitude was an early realization that, real though many of these concerns were, they were more than balanced by the President's attachment to his plan; and that it would be pointless and would do Britain and the transatlantic relationship no good at all if we were seen to be carping and railing at a major American policy move. We had to work with the grain, welcome the proposal and try to fit it into a framework helpful to British and European interests.

It was because of this that the Prime Minister was so irritated by Geoffrey Howe's sceptical speech on SDI to the Royal United Services Institute in March 1985. Technically, it had force; politically, it was unfortunate.

The President's commitment was the major factor in the Prime Minister's reaction. But it was supported by fears of Soviet developments in anti-missile technology, in lasers and anti-particle weapons, fears aroused by her private reading and strengthened by our intelligence reports on the considerable Soviet programme in this field.

Later there was a third consideration, a realization of the strain which competition with the United States in space technology was imposing on the creaking Soviet economy. I recall her agreeing strongly with my suggestion that it was in our interests that the Soviet Union should feel the full economic burden of its conflicting civil and military programmes.

On the more positive and personal side, there was her interest as a scientist in the scheme, encouraged by long talks with General Abrahamson, its director. There were also hopes that British industry would benefit substantially from SDI-related contracts, though in the end the gains proved only modest.

In the first substantial discussions with the President on the subject, at Camp David in December 1984, the objective was therefore to support SDI but to place it, if possible, in a less provocative and destabilizing context. This was achieved by some clever drafting, to which the Americans agreed with only one amendment.

The four-point Camp David statement accepted SDI as a fact (thereby pleasing hardliners in Washington), but drew a line between research and testing on the one hand and deployment on the other (thereby pleasing the State Department and the pragmatists). SDI-related deployments would have to be a matter for negotiations. The object of such negotiations would be to achieve security with reduced levels of offensive weapons on both sides. The US and the West were not seeking to achieve superiority, but to maintain balance, taking account of Soviet developments. The overall aim was to enhance, not to undermine deterrence.

This struck a reassuring balance. By its references to negotiation and deterrence it preserved most of the features of the existing strategic scene. Within this framework SDI was to be pursued primarily as a research programme. Of course this was only temporary relief. The four points could not be a final resting place. US science was unleashed; US officials, characteristically, were taking up varying positions on the aims of the programme and its relation to the ABM Treaty; and the President, who had the engaging capacity of holding conflicting views at the same time, was back within weeks to some of his favourite themes. But the joint statement repaired a dangerous crack between Washington and European capitals and was a marked success for British diplomacy and the Prime Minister personally.

The Russians on the other hand did not find the communiqué at all reassuring. They had reacted immediately and negatively to the President's announcement of SDI in 1983. Their main line of public attack was that it would launch a new arms race and would lead to 'the militarization of space'. Privately, they feared that this space programme, coupled with general American efforts at military modernization, could portend American planning for a first strike. Their military leaders argued that they could not afford to reduce the Soviet offensive armoury while the threat of an elaborate anti-missile screen hung over their heads. The removal, or emasculation, of SDI therefore became a prime object of Soviet policy: Soviet leaders were ready to contemplate arms reduction packages of an increasingly dramatic kind, provided always that President Reagan renounced SDI. This he was adamant that he would not do; he also refused to use the programme as a bargaining counter; though by its very existence, if only as a prospect, it had in fact already become one and was exerting growing pressure on the East-West struggle and on Gorbachev's calculations.

From the Soviet point of view, its most serious effect was to open up a new area of East-West military and technological competition and expenditure at a time when the Soviet economy was already under severe strain and when Gorbachev was desperate to restore life to it by committing maximum resources on the civil side. Over the critical years from 1985 to 1989 this essential breathing-space was denied him, with fatal consequences for the Soviet system.

There was, however, one related theme where the President's hopes and Soviet interests dangerously coincided, namely the abolition of nuclear weapons. For Reagan this was part of his private vision, constantly cropping up in his speeches and in private messages to the Soviet leaders. Strictly speaking, SDI was only a means to this end. For the Russians, it represented a powerful lever with which to shift the military balance in their favour: in Europe overwhelmingly superior Soviet conventional forces and chemical weapons were only balanced by American nuclear weapons and NATO's readiness to use them as part of the 'flexible response' strategy. Deprived of this protection, Western Europe would be rapidly decoupled and neutralized. Moreover in Gorbachev the Soviet Union had acquired a leader who was an adroit tactician, skilled in offering eye-catching proposals aimed at winning over both Western opinion and its appetite for *détente*, while improving the Soviet strategic position. He would seek to present SDI as the one obstacle to a nuclear-free world.

So, while US-Soviet arms discussions ran into the sand because of the clash over SDI, as at Reagan's summit with Gorbachev at Geneva in November 1985, an underground stream of correspondence on nuclear weapons flowed on between the White House and the Kremlin. In January 1986, as part of this interchange, Gorbachev sent a message proposing that both sides eliminate nuclear weapons and ballistic missiles by the year 2000. Later in the year he suggested that he and the President should meet privately for two days as a prelude to his planned visit to Washington.

This was the background to the Reykjavik meeting in October 1986, the most dramatic and confused passage in the superpower dialogue. In a two-day session of private and largely unscripted discussion, Reagan and Gorbachev agreed on massive reductions in intermediate-range weapons, leaving only 100 on each side. More important, they agreed on a 50 per cent reduction over a five-year period of strategic nuclear forces (bombers, long-range Cruise missiles and ballistic missiles); and on the removal of all strategic ballistic missiles within ten years. Gorbachev also proposed, and the President was apparently ready to accept, the elimination of all strategic nuclear weapons within ten years.

There was a catch, however. Gorbachev stipulated that these dramatic changes, which would have swung the military balance markedly in the Soviet favour, should be dependent on American agreement to confine SDI to laboratory work, in effect to kill the programme. The President refused and the summit failed. Gorbachev made it clear that he could not go back to the Politburo after such concessions on offensive weapons without the scalp of SDI. Lacking that, he said, he would be called a dummy, not a leader. He was sincere: it was the standard Russian precondition in a new form. The President for his part would not treat his programme as a bargaining counter.

It seems clear that Gorbachev overplayed his hand. As Dr

Kissinger has pointed out, if the communiqué had announced the agreements on ballistic missiles, leaving the issue of SDI testing for further negotiation, the Russians would have pocketed an immense strategic gain and created a climate in which further US expenditure on SDI was politically impossible.[9] As it was, the programme which had so inspired the President preserved him from an historic blunder.

The news of Reykjavik caused us great alarm in London. An agreement along the lines proposed would have upset the deterrent balance and left Western Europe exposed to preponderant Soviet conventional forces and chemical weapons. NATO would have been fractured. The old European nightmare, of a US-Soviet deal over their heads, would have been realized. In addition, the British and French deterrents would have become unsustainable: a different system would have had to be found, but in an anti-nuclear climate which would effectively rule out public support for the heavy expenditure involved.

It was not only the magnitude of the changes contemplated that was so disturbing; it was the almost insouciant way in which, as it seemed, the President and his senior officials had embarked on such high-risk horse-trading. The full consequences had not been thought through; the allies had not been consulted. Afterwards, American experts recovered their senses and began to point out the risks for the West of a world without nuclear weapons. But that was rather late in the day. There was also the worrying thought that the Reykjavik thinking might recur in future summits, with unpredictable results.

As she reveals in her memoirs, the Prime Minister was badly shaken. She decided to fly to Washington, and together with Charles Powell I sat with her the day before to work out the arguments she would deploy. The prime object of the mission had to be to extract from the President a public endorsement of the principle that reductions in nuclear weapons must take account of imbalances in conventional and chemical weapons and that for the foreseeable future the Alliance would continue to depend on nuclear deterrence. In return, the Prime Minister was ready to welcome an agreement on intermediate-range missiles and a 50 per cent cut over five years in US and Soviet strategic offensive weapons.

To that everything else was secondary. But we also had to be ready to point out that if ballistic missiles were abolished, Cruise missiles and bombers would not be able to carry the weight of deterrence: they had less capacity to survive, less penetration and less range. Nor was there any prospect of paying for the vast increases in conventional forces and chemical weapons that would be needed to meet Soviet superiority in those fields once the Alliance's nuclear armoury was abolished. And so on. It was a very thorough and urgent briefing session.

In the event, the President, face to face with the Prime Minister, proved more amenable than we had feared and readily took her points. This was a vast relief, but at the same time disturbing, for it suggested that his original position had not been the product of very thorough reflection. The second Camp David statement agreed to give priority to an agreement on intermediate-range missiles, a 50 per cent cut over five years in US and Soviet strategic weapons, and a ban on chemical weapons. The SDI research programme was to be pursued within the terms of the ABM Treaty. In the key passage the two leaders confirmed that NATO's strategy would continue to require effective nuclear deterrence based on a mix of systems; and any reductions in nuclear weapons would increase the importance of eliminating conventional disparities. A stable overall balance was needed at all times. The President reaffirmed the US intention of proceeding with his strategic modernization programme, including Trident. He also confirmed his full support for the arrangements made to modernize Britain's independent nuclear deterrent with Trident.

This was as good a result as could possibly have been expected. Once again the Prime Minister's intervention had restored strategic stability and Alliance cohesion. But this was a bigger achievement than the first Camp David meeting, in part because the danger had been greater, in part because of the serious impact of last-minute failure on the Russians. The SDI programme continued; and the economic pressures on Gorbachev mounted. Before long the agreed cuts in intermediate-range and strategic weapons which had been tied to the shackling of SDI came without that rider; and by the end of 1988 Gorbachev was offering major reductions in conventional forces on a unilateral basis.

The vision of a non-nuclear world receded and became again a remote aspiration. The idea of eliminating ballistic missiles altogether was quietly buried by the Joint Chiefs of Staff, who pointed out the immense cost of restructuring American defences to ensure adequate protection on that basis. Faint traces of Reykjavik lingered in the communiqués at the end of the year. But by May 1987 the doctrine of nuclear deterrence was fully restored; and the West was back in the position the Prime Minister and her advisers wanted: that is, a united Alliance watching and encouraging from a position of strength the changes occurring on the other side of the East-West fault-line.

SDI, the catalyst which had provoked and then helped overcome these crises, had a later chequered career. With President Reagan gone and the Soviet Union falling apart, it looked less necessary and US funding was reduced. It had always had its enemies in Congress. The vision behind it grew more modest: rather than a comprehensive shield it became a means of protecting certain installations against a Soviet first strike. As such, it diminished into an adjunct of conventional deterrence.

The Gulf War and the sight of Patriot missiles defending Israel against Saddam Hussein's rockets revived American interest and I recall US officials explaining to Stephen Wall (John Major's Private Secretary) and myself the new system, known as GOPALS (global protection against limited strikes). This again was a scaled-down version of the original; but it was thought of as capable of giving protection to cities rather than just military installations.

With another change of President in 1992, again the funding was reduced and US attachment to the ABM Treaty reaffirmed. The Star Wars vision of country-wide defence against strategic ballistic missiles has been buried. But the idea of missile defence of a more circumscribed kind is very much alive. The emergence of maverick states with missile technology and weapons of mass destruction gives it a continuing, and strengthening, *raison d'être*. Whatever happens, the philosophy of defence has already had its moment of history as an instrument in the collapse of the Soviet Union.

9

The United States:
The Raid on Libya and Irangate

THE YEAR 1986 was pre-eminently that of Reykjavik. But it was also the year of the US raid on Libya and the year of Irangate. Both episodes tested the alliance in their different ways.

The raid on Libya was another of those sudden, unilateral acts in the style of Grenada. In this case there was, happily, some notice and consultation; but the policy choices were again painful.

The background was the growing involvement of Colonel Gaddafi's government in terrorism in a period heavily marked by Middle East terrorist incidents. State-sponsored terrorism was the fashionable trend; and Libya, Syria and Iran were the prime culprits. In August 1984 we helped sweep Libyan mines laid in the Red Sea. As our researches showed, Libya and Syria were implicated in a bomb explosion at Frankfurt international airport in June 1985. Libya was responsible for a car bomb at a US airbase at Rhein-Main in August 1985. Libya had a hand in the hijacking of the Italian cruise ship, *Achille Lauro*, in October 1985, in the course of which an American Jewish passenger was murdered. In December 1985 terrorist attacks at Rome and Vienna airports by the Abu Nidhal organization with Libyan support caused heavy loss of life. Gaddafi described the attacks as heroic.

Earlier, in April 1984, Britain had been directly involved when a policewoman, Yvonne Fletcher, was killed by shots from the Libyan mission in St James's Square.

Colonel Gaddafi therefore had a distinguished track record. There was shared Anglo-American concern over his intentions, plus a quantity of intelligence about his activities. The difficulty was to know what to do. As far as government responsibility went, the attacks were Libyan at second hand only: international law would find it hard to justify Western military action against Libya on those grounds alone. But the US Administration, understandably, was not content to remain inactive, or to allow a state to evade its international responsibilities by employing surrogates. In January 1986 President Reagan warned that if Libya used terrorists to attack US citizens, that would be regarded as an attack by regular Libyan forces, calling for an appropriate military reply. He also announced that the United States was severing all economic ties with Libya. There was US pressure for more general economic sanctions, including a ban on Libyan oil, but this met with little enthusiasm. European countries did considerable business with Libya and there was a sizeable British business community there.

In March 1986 the quarrel escalated. The US navy held exercises in disputed waters in the Gulf of Sirte, on the northern coast of Libya; and when the Libyans fired missiles at US planes it replied by sinking two Libyan patrol boats and damaging an anti-aircraft battery. In response Gaddafi announced a state of war with the United States and threatened all US NATO bases.

On 5 April a bomb exploded in La Belle discothèque in Berlin, a favourite haunt of US servicemen. Two people were killed, one an American soldier. Over 200, including 50 Americans, were injured. Intelligence made it clear that the Libyans were responsible.

The US Administration now moved fast. On Tuesday, 8 April, President Reagan sent a personal message to Mrs Thatcher, seeking permission to use F-111 planes and support aircraft based in Britain in air attacks on Libya. British-based aircraft were not essential; but, flying from bases nearer at hand, they would assure greater accuracy and greater pilot safety. We were asked for an early reply.

I recall being summoned to No. 10 late that evening. An interim reply was prepared. We were not entirely surprised; but we were worried. The request was far from precise and we were not sure that the Administration had thought through the consequences. We took a gloomier view than they did of the likely repercussions in the Arab world; and we did not like the prospect of becoming wholly identified with the US position in that most sensitive of areas. Above all, there were British hostages in Lebanon. The reply expressed general support but posed a series of questions.

The American reply was brisk and rather tough. They were going ahead and they discounted our fears of Arab reactions. (In this, as it turned out, they were right.) This time the President was more specific about targets, that is Gaddafi's headquarters and the offices of the Libyan security and intelligence apparatus, in other words, objectives directly related to terrorist operations. We now had to consider our substantive reply in the knowledge that the raid would take place in any event.

As she explains in her memoirs, the Prime Minister's strong instinct was to meet the President's request. America was our closest ally, on whom we depended for our ultimate security. We had to agree. But there was the question of legality. As recently as January, she had gone on record condemning retaliatory strikes. At first sight, the operation proposed fell exactly into that category.

Among the small group of ministers and officials who sat with the Prime Minister to handle the issue the Attorney-General, Michael Havers, naturally stressed the importance of showing that any moves we made fell within the ambit of Article 51 of the United Nations Charter, permitting military action in self-defence. It was, I think, the Defence Secretary, George Younger, who suggested we combine a 'Yes' reply with a reference to self-defence. I argued that this could square our particular circle: fortunately we had enough evidence from intelligence not only of Libyan responsibility for the bomb at the Berlin discothèque, but also of their instructions for other terrorist enterprises. In other words we were in a continuum of terrorist activity and had the right to defend ourselves against coming dangers.

The reply sent pledged support but emphasized the need for the President to set his response within the context of self-defence rather than retaliation. It underlined the importance of keeping the targets as narrowly related to terrorism as possible; and it added a warning of the difficulties we would have in backing more wide-ranging action.

The American raid took place a few days later, on 14 April, amid much pre-publicity. It was not entirely surgical: there were some civilian casualties and one American aircraft was lost. But it left a much subdued Gaddafi: there was no massive Libyan retaliation; and by demonstrating that the US government was prepared to take strong measures against state-sponsored terrorism, the operation had a valuable deterrent effect in the Middle East as a whole.

But, as had been feared, our hostages suffered: tragically, two were executed, almost certainly at Libyan behest, in the days following the raid. And valuable intelligence sources were lost: it was impossible to explain our confidence in Libyan responsibility without compromising them. Even so, I came under some criticism for my inability to provide a more sensational account of Gaddafi's record for government speakers to use: the knowledge was there, but too highly classified.

Britain alone had said yes to the American request. The French government would not allow the F-111s to overfly French territory, forcing them into a long detour. The Spaniards were likewise uncooperative and the Germans critical.

British public opinion was also critical, highly so. The raid had been reported in emotional terms, with emphasis on the civilian casualties. There was even – a rare event – doubt and some dissatisfaction expressed by ministers when the Overseas and Defence Committee of the Cabinet was informed of the decision, though this had more to do with the lack of consultation than with the substance of the case.

By contrast, there was warm applause and gratitude throughout the United States for our response and the Prime Minister's stock there reached new heights. Among the identifiable gains was congressional approval for the new extradition treaty, enabling the return to Britain of IRA terrorists held in America. There were other benefits in terms of access and influence of a less easily measurable kind.

The Libyan raid was a good example of one aspect of the US-UK relationship in the Reagan-Thatcher years: an active, assertive Administration, determined to use American power in response to terrorism and not too concerned with the niceties of international law; a more cautious British partner, ideally preferring a less exposed position, but firm on the primacy of the US connection. The decision taken was a difficult one, with real cost to us, particularly in British lives. But I am sure it was right.

There was a sequel. Our agreement to the President's request had made it clear that our support for further American action could not be taken for granted; and the domestic reaction to the raid underlined the wisdom of this reservation. But we wondered whether further US action might not be on the way. In particular we wondered about Syria, another terrorist state, implicated in many of the incidents of the time, and a haven for Abu Nidhal, probably the most dangerous terrorist organization in the Middle East. Another request for the use of planes from US bases in Britain would have been politically very delicate. Even without that, a US attack which we would have been expected to applaud might be awkward. At the least, we needed good notice. I argued that as a precaution we should encourage bilateral discussions with Washington on terrorism, which should at least give us foreknowledge and influence at an early stage. The Prime Minister agreed that the experts on each side should exchange assessments and that Sir Antony Acland, the Permanent Under-Secretary at the Foreign Office, and I should visit Washington to discuss the aftermath of the Libyan episode.

Fortunately, we found the Americans in a sober mood, not disposed to make exaggerated claims about the effect of their strike and inclined to favour concerted European non-military measures as a way of keeping up the pressure. We could be reasonably confident that, short of some further major and identifiable outrage, with loss of American lives, there would be no early Act II in Libya.

Syria was a different proposition, tougher, more influential, more discreet: an unlikely target. Syria was, however, vulnerable to diplomatic pressure because it aspired to function as a conventional and respectable Middle East state; and we agreed that there would be merit in Western governments bringing home to the Syrians the contradiction between that ambition and their shady record as a state harbouring and running terrorists. This was a reassuring outcome.

At the end of our visit Antony Acland and I called on the newly appointed National Security Adviser, Admiral Poindexter. We ran over the Middle East scene with him and told him of the political problems further US military action would present the other Europeans and ourselves. We also went on to say that any deal over hostages that was seen as profiting the hostage-takers would greatly weaken the Western stand over terrorism.

The background to this last Delphic comment was provided by growing rumours that the United States might after all be engaged in some such hostage deal. It would be wrong to claim that we in London were wholly ignorant: we had picked up indications that something odd was going on. But they were fragmentary; and the knowledge, such as it was, was almost unusable. Apart from making the most general comments about solidarity in the face of terrorism, we had to lock it away and await the inevitable leak.

It came in November of that year with revelations in a Beirut newspaper. The story, and, sadly, the facts, were that some elements of the US government had been engaged for some time in attempted deals with Iran for the release of US hostages in return for the sale to Iran of anti-tank weapons. It later transpired that this was a triangular arrangement and that the funds generated by the weapons sales were being applied to support the cause of the Contra rebels fighting the Sandinista government in Nicaragua. Here was an outsize can of worms. The formidable investigative apparatus of the American Congress and media was let loose upon it.

For us in London it was very bad news. To put it mildly, the policy unearthed did not sit well with the Western code of conduct towards terrorism adopted as recently as the Tokyo economic summit in May 1986. Among the measures agreed there was a 'refusal to export arms to states which sponsor or support terrorism'. Western solidarity and credibility on a central policy issue were thereby undermined. Western neutrality in the Iraq-Iran War was compromised. The Prime Minister was put in an embarrassing position, though she handled it skilfully on her visit to Washington later in November, confining herself to repeated expressions of confidence in the President's personal integrity.

But most serious was the likely impact on US policy and authority. Secretary Shultz endeavoured to reassure NATO foreign ministers in Brussels in December: 'The going will be rough; but the President and his policies will stay in place.' This was all very well, but we recalled the effect of an administration in disarray during the final years of the Nixon presidency. In early 1987 I minuted the Prime Minister that there were two issues overhanging the international scene: the aftermath of Reykjavik and the weakening of the President.

We had to consider whether the effect of the revelations would be to drive the Administration into some demonstration of strength, perhaps another attack on a Middle East state, or even an attempt, which would almost certainly fail, to rescue US hostages in Lebanon. Or would they in compensation be too eager for a popular arms agreement with the Russians? And, by the same token, would not the Russians become more demanding? The analogy of President Nixon, wounded by Watergate, hastening to Moscow in the summer of 1974 was not encouraging. And, despite the agreed statement at Camp David the preceding November, might not the President now be tempted over ballistic missiles or nuclear weapons, if offered the chance of an historic accomplishment before leaving office? In any event, the timetable for congressional hearings and reports seemed certain to extend the agony well into 1987.

As it turned out, these fears proved exaggerated and the President recovered sooner than at first seemed possible. He was better established in American affections than Nixon had been. His readiness to delegate, his inattention to detail proved helpful. A more organized man would have been more vulnerable. His own simple, though hardly explicable, conviction that he had never traded arms for hostages could not be dented. Secretary Shultz, relatively unscathed by Irangate, remained in steady charge of East-West diplomacy; and the thaw there, partly the result of Gorbachev's restlessness, partly the result of the economic pressures on the Soviet Union, made possible solid achievements in arms reduction: 1987, which had opened as the year of a discredited President, ended with a US-Soviet summit in Washington and a major treaty on intermediate-range missiles.

10

The United States:
The Anchor to Windward

Throughout the Reagan presidency Britain was visibly the most important and influential of America's allies. The fact was underlined by high-profile prime ministerial visits to Washington and by communiqués of much more than bilateral significance issuing from them. British interventions helped shape the East-West strategic dialogue and Britain took the lead in contacts with the new regime in Moscow, where Mrs Thatcher's 1987 visit was the forerunner and in some sense the guide to President Reagan's visit a year later. In crises outside the NATO area, as over Libya, Britain and America were usually to be found together, with our European partners straggling away in postures of greater detachment, or even dissent.

But this was a position which we were unable to sustain. After 1988, with a new administration in Washington, British influence, though still substantial, declined; and in more relaxed conditions in Central Europe British diplomacy for the first time began to appear less sensitive and effective than it might have been. The shift was illustrated by the debate within the Alliance over short-range missiles.

The idea of an agreement drastically reducing intermediate-range missiles (INF) had been one of the welter flung up at Reykjavik. At that time the Russians made it conditional on the emasculation of the Strategic Defense Initiative. But it re-emerged as a free-standing proposal in the spring of 1987 during Secretary of State Shultz's visit to Moscow. Its scope and precise terms remained uncertain until later in the year: would it cover only the longer-range group of weapons, those from 1,000 to 5,500 kilometres, or be extended to the shorter-range, from 500 to 1,000 kilometres? And would it require reduction to zero, or would it permit a small number of missiles to be retained outside Europe, in Soviet Asia and in Alaska? In the end it was agreed that it would cover both groups and that it would impose a double zero.

The INF Treaty, signed in Washington in December 1987, was therefore simple and dramatic. For the first time a whole category of weapons, and nuclear weapons at that, was abolished. Verification was thereby made easier; and verification of an altogether more rigorous and intrusive kind than before was a feature of the treaty. Moreover, since the Soviet Union had many more of the missiles in question than the West, there was an immediate apparent security gain.

The treaty was by any standards a major achievement in arms reduction, the first step in the transformation of the military and political scene in Europe that was to take place over the next few years. But there were longer-term concerns. The removal of a wide range of nuclear weapons in the European theatre would leave Western Europe more exposed to the immensely superior Soviet conventional forces, hitherto balanced only by Western nuclear capacity. These forces also possessed chemical weapons in quantity and were well rehearsed in their battlefield use. Again, the only Western answer was nuclear. Western security also rested on the capacity for flexible response, the ability to hit back at a series of levels against possible attacks from the East. Now several rungs in the ladder would be removed: at one end there would be nuclear weapons with ranges of less than 500 kilometres; at the other intercontinental missiles. NATO's response would become less proportionate and thereby less credible.

By concentrating his arms reduction proposals on the nuclear side Gorbachev was moving steadily towards a European balance favourable to his country. Moreover the superficial popularity of his initiatives, the success of his charm offensive, made it harder for anyone to sound a cautionary note about the path we were treading. Western governments were becoming less ready to believe that the Soviet Union presented any threat; but this was happening at the same time as Soviet diplomacy was proving unusually adept; and at a time when the Soviet Foreign Minister was cleverly proposing a new round of negotiations on reducing short-range nuclear forces (SNF). This was an idea calculated to divide NATO; if accepted, it would be likely to lead to a third zero and a shift in the European balance of forces in the Soviet favour.

The Prime Minister was very alive to these dangers and I shared her worries. The post-INF Treaty landscape was not, as some of our allies were inclined to think, the Promised Land. At her prompting, the United States agreed to assign more sea-launched Cruise missiles and F-111 aircraft to NATO to compensate for the loss of Pershing and ground-launched Cruise; but there was no substitute for ground-launched weapons as a means of marking the American commitment to the defence of Europe. In their absence there was inevitably doubt about the American response to a Soviet attack and greater risk of decoupling.

To safeguard the overall balance there would now have to be agreements to reduce conventional and chemical weapons. By definition these would have to be asymmetrical agreements. But conventional arms negotiations had been going on for years at Vienna without real progress; they had become as technical and sterile as disputations between medieval schoolmen. Vienna was a comfortable posting but hardly the site for active arms reduction. As for chemical weapons, a convention would be relatively simple to draft but virtually impossible to police: such weapons were alarmingly easy for any industrial state to manufacture and conceal.

The effect of these considerations was to place great weight, more as it turned out than the shaky political structure could bear, on the remaining lower rungs in the ladder of flexible response, that is on NATO's short-range weapons. As we saw it in London, they must be retained; there must be no third zero; and they must be modernized where necessary: the existing short-range LANCE missile would soon need a successor and a tactical air-to-surface missile (TASM) would be needed to take the place of the existing free-fall bombs. On the other side, the Russians had many more missiles in the short range than NATO (1,400 as against 88) and they had recently modernized their armoury.

What we sought therefore was a clear understanding with our allies that SNF constituted an irreducible minimum in Western defences and that there could be no negotiations for their reduction until we had reached a balance over conventional forces and chemical weapons.

These were entirely logical propositions. Unfortunately they underestimated the political pressures on one key ally, Germany. As the range of the weapons at issue diminished, the spotlight fell more and more on Germany. A shift in the European military balance in favour of the Soviet Union could well mean a neutral Germany; for Moscow that had always been the great prize. It was in Germany that the short-range missiles were stationed; and it was between the two Germanies that any exchange of fire would take place. The West German government began by being very robust, but as time passed and *détente à la Gorbachev* gathered momentum, found it increasingly hard to accept that the only category of land-based nuclear weapons in Europe to be retained and modernized should be those on German soil.

Against this background Chancellor Kohl's discussions with the Prime Minister became increasingly unsatisfactory from our point of view. Personal relations between the two leaders had never been ideal and the Prime Minister's arguments and strictures became more severe as the Chancellor and Herr Genscher, his Foreign Minister, grew more evasive.

The other decisive factor in the equation was of course Washington's attitude. Here too we began to sense a disturbing ambiguity. In her talks with President Reagan in 1987 and 1988 about the implications of the INF Treaty, the Prime Minister had found him solid on the need to maintain and modernize NATO's short-range missiles and on the importance of avoiding East-West negotiation for the reduction of this category until we had parity on conventional forces and a ban on chemical weapons. Her discussions with James Baker, the new Secretary of State, in late 1988 left her with a similar impression. But the German position was weakening. They were apparently ready to contemplate SNF negotiations and were unconvinced of the need for modernization. If their view was to be countered and the Alliance's defences maintained the British and US positions would have to be identical and firm.

At this point, late in the day and just before the NATO summit, it transpired that the US position was far from firm. They had moved and were now prepared to accept the principle of SNF negotiations, leaving Britain as the only NATO member opposed, apart from the special case of France. This was an unenviable position for the Prime Minister. She was saved from public embarrassment by a clever, eleventh-hour American proposal for rapid cuts in conventional forces. This enabled the Alliance to sidestep the issue of SNF modernization. It also enabled the Germans to claim that early SNF negotiations were still in prospect.

It was a face-saving compromise, but one which leaned more in the German direction than the British. The Prime Minister could point out in the Commons that there would be no negotiations to reduce short-range missiles until an agreement on a reduction in conventional forces was concluded and in the course of implementation. But the fact remained that the normal close consultation between London and Washington had not taken place and that Germany had apparently carried more weight in US councils than had Britain.

In a speech at Mainz a few days after the NATO summit President Bush spoke of the Germans as 'partners in leadership', which seemed to rub the point in. Privately, he commended Britain's role in the argument as 'the anchor to windward', without which a solution would not have been possible. This was kindly meant but was not exactly reassuring: the anchor to windward is a lonely position and not the one we had imagined we occupied.

From our point of view, it had not been a very successful

episode; but it was salutary. It reminded us of the changing of the guard in Washington and of the fact that we could not expect to carry the easy understanding of the Reagan era automatically through into the new regime. The retiring President had endeavoured to ensure continuity by inviting Mrs Thatcher to Washington as his final guest in November 1988, when she would also be able to meet his successor. But Bush and Baker were different personalities from Reagan and Shultz; and George Bush, making the giant stride between the Vice-Presidency and the White House, not surprisingly felt the need to draw a line between the two presidencies and show that he was not to be taken for granted. Though the two got on well, the relationship between him and the Prime Minister was never quite as comfortable as with his predecessor. It took a little time for her to adjust. She was also paying the price for her success in the last eight years: her interventions and her weight in US deliberations had naturally aroused some resentment among those on the losing side in the arguments. There were now new players and a new style.

But there was another factor, of even greater significance for the future. Not only was the Soviet Union changing under the impact, intended or unintended, of Gorbachev's reforms; the Central European situation was changing as the East-West dialogue quickened. Old rigidities were beginning to soften; new possibilities were emerging; and in this new, more fluid setting the importance of Germany was rapidly growing. It was also growing in the estimation of the new administration in Washington, who were inclined to think in terms of an integrated Europe, not the instinctive approach to European issues at No. 10.

These were disturbing signs. As I argued, we needed to catch up with the game and get back to the centre of the Alliance. That meant not only talking the issues through with President Bush but also reassessing our relations with Bonn. We had argued with irreproachable military logic but with less than perfect political sense. The lessons were there, but, as it turned out, we were unable to apply them.

I I

The Soviet Union: Before the Flood

WE KNOW A great deal about the Soviet Union these days, the 'old Soviet Union', or the 'former Soviet Union', as it should more accurately be called; a great deal about its elaborate tyranny, its falsified history, its sclerotic economy, its ecological disasters, its enslaved minorities, its corruption, inefficiency and general impracticality. So much that, with our present hindsight, it often seems that such a system could scarcely have existed, that it could only have been a bad dream which would fade and dissolve at the approach of day and the light of human reason. But history contains many things that outrage reason and we have to remind ourselves that the Soviet Union was for long an enormous fact, which at first engaged the ideals and hopes of many of the most enlightened in the West and which, when the vision lost its glow and truth began to dawn, still preoccupied Western leaders as the embodiment of the collectivist challenge to their free-market system, and which then, in its final manifestation, remained, until a few years ago, an overwhelming military threat.

We have to step back in time and shed our modern knowledge, our wisdom after the event. As part of that effort it may be helpful to describe how the Soviet Union appeared to a Western observer at the beginning of 1984, which was the time I took up my post at No. 10.

The outstanding fact about the Soviet Union then was that it was a formidable and hostile military superpower. At a low estimate,

86

some 15 per cent of its gross national product was devoted to military spending. According to many yardsticks, it looked militarily stronger than the United States. It had one-third more land-based intercontinental ballistic missiles and was ahead in the business of making them mobile and therefore less vulnerable. It was building ballistic missile submarines and long-range bombers much faster than the Americans. It held large stocks of chemical and biological weapons. It threatened Western Europe not only with long-range missiles, but also, as explained above, with the new class of intermediate-range SS20s, posing particularly acute problems for European defence. In addition, it enjoyed a vast superiority in conventional arms. Warsaw Pact forces west of the Urals numbered 165 divisions in the early 1970s and rose to nearly 190 in 1986. The forward-deployed divisions in Eastern Europe were far more numerous than could conceivably be needed for defence; they enjoyed a superiority over NATO in offensive weapons (tanks and artillery) of more than two to one; and they were highly trained and regularly exercised in offensive operations.

In the Third World, the Russians or their surrogates were established at various points in Africa, Asia and Central America. Russian forces had invaded Afghanistan in 1979, raising the possibility of further southward expansion. A fast-growing Soviet navy and air-transport arm projected Soviet power across the globe.

There were at the time no on-going arms negotiations, bringing the two camps into regular contact and reducing the risk of misreading and miscalculation. The Russians had left the talks on intermediate weapons and those on strategic weapons. As we now know, the Soviet leaders were sufficiently paranoid to fear a sudden attack by the West and even to suspect that a particular NATO exercise might provide the cover for such preparations. In September 1983 a Korean airliner which had strayed into Soviet airspace was shot down by a Soviet fighter with the loss of 269 lives, including 62 Americans. The Russians made no apology.

The atmosphere was therefore tense and superpower communication minimal. There was little difficulty in concluding that the

Soviet Union constituted the principal threat to the West: the difficulty lay more in assessing how serious and how lasting a threat and
in defining its main direction. Soviet successes in the Third World,
though sometimes striking, seemed to me of secondary significance. Except in areas contiguous to the Soviet Union and directly
accessible to Soviet land forces, they were inherently unstable, as
the Soviet expulsion from Egypt in 1972 had demonstrated.

Much more serious was the threat to Western Europe. It was not
so much the risk of an actual Soviet attack, though in prudence this
could never be discounted and NATO planning had to reckon with
it. It was more the danger that, lacking vigilance and constancy on
our part and that of our allies, Soviet military strength could cast
such a shadow over West European governments that their policies
would increasingly take account of and reflect Soviet wishes. The
search for a dominant influence over the western tip of the
Eurasian landmass seemed to me a constant in Russian policy,
whether under Tsarist or Communist leaders.

There was of course the question of the Soviet economy. This
had been the object of exaggerated Western fears in the 1960s. In
October 1961, in one of his election debates with Nixon, Kennedy
had said that, according to CIA estimates, Soviet economic growth
was two or three times as great as America's. In the same year he told
Macmillan that the Russians had a buoyant economy and would
soon outmatch capitalism in the race for wealth. Macmillan seems
to have concurred with this assessment and to have said much the
same thing to others. In the 1970s the Soviet figures began to turn
down, but the decline was masked by the upsurge in oil prices as a
result of the Middle East crises of that time. Here the Soviet Union
was a major beneficiary. The sudden flow of money disguised the
urgent need for economic reform and may have encouraged
Brezhnev in Third World adventures strictly beyond his means.

To Western analysts in the early and mid-1980s the growing
weakness of the Soviet economy and the appalling quality of
Soviet life were well known. But there was the balancing fact that
this creaking base supported the apparatus of a serious military
threat. It may have been, as someone said, a case of Upper Volta

with rockets (though a much enlarged Upper Volta with vast resources of men and raw materials); but the rockets were there, in growing numbers and of steadily improving quality; and the military-industrial complex enjoyed the power to ensure that resources continued to be funneled in their direction.

In the end it boiled down to a judgement of the will of Soviet leaders to continue in the traditional way. In 1984 the will seemed unimpaired. Moreover the Kremlin had the ability, denied to democratic governments, of steadily following a set course, untroubled by volatile public opinion. As one celebrated nineteenth-century observer had pointed out, in the foreign policy context 'A democracy can only with great difficulty regulate the details of an important undertaking, persevere in a fixed design, and work out its execution in spite of obstacles. It cannot combine its measures with secrecy or await their consequences with patience.'[10]

And there seemed serious reason to question the steadfastness of the West European democracies in the face of pressure from the Soviet Union and the demands of their domestic constituencies. Were they ready to resist Soviet threats or the attractions of *détente* on Soviet terms? Were they ready to support the necessary expenditure on arms? At the time no one could be confident. As it turned out, it was the Soviet will that cracked. Or rather a leader appeared who thought he could both sustain and radically reform the system.

But this is looking ahead. At the time the concept of an economically flawed but militarily formidable state overhanging Western Europe and constantly striving to tip the balance of power further in its direction underlay most of my minutes to the Prime Minister and accorded readily with her own thinking.

The policy conclusions to be drawn from such an assessment were the need for Western military strength and political constancy, and the urgent requirement for Western economic recovery and further technological advance. But by themselves these were not enough. At the same time contact had to be maintained with the Soviet and the East European governments, not with exaggerated expectations, but so that each side would come to know the other better and so that we could seek a balance of security at a lower level of armaments. Following a Chequers seminar in September 1983, Mrs Thatcher had agreed to a slightly more forward line than had been the case in her first years in office. She decided to visit Hungary, in some ways the most independent and sophisticated of the East European economies, in an attempt to explore the East European situation and perhaps exploit the gaps between Soviet and satellite thinking. She also began to think of a point of contact in the Soviet Union itself. Soviet leaders were ailing and dying in quick succession at the time: the most able, Andropov, died in February 1984; Chernenko, who followed him, succumbed in March 1985. The Prime Minister attended both their funerals and began examining the short-lists of those who might come in as representatives of a younger generation and, with luck, hold power for some time.

It was in this way that an invitation was issued to Mikhail Gorbachev. For once (our record at picking winners had not been good) we drew the right card. Gorbachev, still only the heir presumptive, was pleased with the invitation. He had not had a chance to visit a European capitalist country and it seems likely that his successful trip to Britain helped him in the leadership stakes.

At lunch during the visit to Chequers I sat next to Yakovlev, the former Ambassador to Canada, whom Anatoly Dobrynin, the long-serving Soviet ambassador in Washington, in his memoirs calls 'Gorbachev's evil master-mind'. I had little chance to explore these mental recesses, for conversation at the table was dominated by the opening exchanges in the debate between the Prime Minister and her principal guest, a discussion to be continued in the coming years over many hours in Moscow and London to the great pleasure and profit of both.

12

The Soviet Union:
The Course of Reform

FOR WESTERN GOVERNMENTS the Soviet Union in Gorbachev's early days presented a fascinating exercise in assessment and speculation. He was clearly a vigorous new leader. He was also a reformer; but how serious and thorough? After all, Russia, pre- and post-revolution, had known reform before, always authoritarian, always partial, alternating with periods of conformity and stagnation, as in recent times Khrushchev had been succeeded by Brezhnev. Would the new reforms be able to revitalize the ailing economy? Would there be a political component? And how could that be reconciled with the leading role of the Soviet Communist Party? Above all, what would be the impact on the outside world? This was the aspect that most concerned us. The West could do little to influence the Soviet internal situation but was the direct recipient and even, in one sense, the co-former of Soviet foreign policy.

Gorbachev began gently, following in the steps of his mentor, Andropov. His first slogan was '*uskorenie*', acceleration. He called for tighter labour discipline, faster growth, greater effort, stronger incentives, stricter accounting. He passed decrees curbing the sale of alcohol – measures which did little to stop drunkenness but cost the state much money in lost taxes. This all looked like the mixture as before, though with greater drive and energy.

But by April 1985 he was calling for restructuring (*perestroika*) of the economic mechanism. '*Glasnost*', or openness, came a little later. By the 27th Party Congress in February 1986 *perestroika* was to be extended to a variety of institutions and it was conceded that radical economic reform was necessary. Gorbachev publicly condemned the paralysis of the Brezhnev era and its illusion of 'improving matters without changing anything'. He also attacked in surprisingly bitter terms the obstruction his reforms were apparently already encountering throughout the managerial strata.

The pace was quickening. In January 1987, in a major speech to the Central Committee Plenum, he spoke of the need for political change and prescribed democratization, evidently in an effort to win rank-and-file support and thereby outflank his senior bureaucratic opponents. He now attributed the problems of the Soviet system not just to the locust years under Brezhnev but to fundamental defects in the Soviet model. The disease had proved more deep-seated than at first supposed and the remedies had to be correspondingly drastic. This escalation, more difficulties, more reform, was to be a recurrent feature of the next few years.

In June 1987 the Plenum of the Central Committee adopted a 'law on the socialist enterprise' which explicitly admitted the need to incorporate market reforms; and Gorbachev stated that the Soviet Union had to achieve 'the systematic mastery and management of the market, with due regard for its laws and the strengthening and increase in the power of the rouble'.[11]

This was a remarkable admission. Yet Gorbachev repeatedly made it plain that he was a devout believer in the socialist system. He was not trying to break the mould. His democratization had nothing in common with bourgeois democracy. He wanted a revivified and strengthened Soviet Union, able to enter the twenty-first century 'in a manner befitting a great power':

Some people have been suggesting things that go beyond the bounds of our system, and in particular that we abandon the instrument of the planned economy. We have not gone down that road and will never do so, because we are getting ready to strengthen socialism and not to replace it with a different system.[12]

Here was the paradox of the sincere but partial reformer engineering a major thaw in the frozen Soviet landscape, but still convinced that the main features of that landscape should and could be retained. Behind this confidence, and running through the whole of Gorbachev's reforms, was a deep *naïveté*, a belief that he could release the immense forces imprisoned by a dictatorship and yet remain in control, an unwillingness or inability to recognize that in the end there was no middle way between Party rule on the one hand and popular government on the other.

Yet it was becoming clear that, of the consequences of his measures, the unintended were at least as important as the intended. The new openness and the encouragement of intellectual freedom, designed to generate enthusiasm for reform as decreed from above, in fact prompted a much deeper and more destructive self-analysis. Particularly after the Party conference in the summer of 1987, ministers and intellectuals vied with one another in public admissions of the poverty, stagnation and backwardness of Soviet society: the low life expectancy, the primitive state of the infrastructure, the lack of proper educational facilities, the failure of Soviet science, the absurdity of the economic system. To a population reared in the dogma of the inherent and inevitable superiority of socialism the admissions were devastating.

As one Russian economist put it: 'We are now like a seriously ill man who, after a long time in bed, takes his first step with the greatest difficulty and finds, to his horror, that he has almost forgotten how to walk.'[13] In essence, the message was that the Soviet system did not work. The model had failed.

Nor was it only Russians who were making themselves heard. Ethnic minorities across the Union were seizing on the new opportunities for self-expression to present petitions and demands for the redress of national injustices and in some cases going beyond that to embark on violent demonstrations and racial clashes. The dangerously heterogeneous nature of the state, with 51 per cent of its population non-Russian, was being exposed; and its leader was facing an increasingly sharp contradiction between his need to maintain Moscow's central control and his wish to encourage greater freedom and participation among the non-Russian republics.

There was a third aspect to the new frankness. After some initial hesitation on the part of government and intelligentsia, it was exploited to turn back the pages of Soviet history and cast light on its darker places. The reform process was seen to need a basis in intellectual honesty. Stalin came under increasingly thorough condemnation. His victims, like Bukharin, were formally rehabilitated. Even Lenin, hitherto sacrosanct, was examined by the historians and found wanting.

Whatever else Gorbachev was doing, he was, unwittingly but effectively, destroying the historical, ideological and, if the word can be used in such a context, the moral foundations of the Soviet system.

Following this accelerating tide of change and advising on our policy reactions was an exciting but demanding business. As I saw it, Gorbachev had probably embarked on an impossible enterprise, in the sense that he would be unable to reach his twin goals of revitalizing and at the same time preserving the system he had inherited. But the manner and timing of his failure were impossible to predict. Eventually he might be displaced. But removing the Soviet General Secretary was no easy matter; and he displayed not only a growing appetite for reform, but also considerable agility and tactical skill in defending his position. It would be wise to assume he would have a long ride, even with a highly uncertain outcome. During that time his reforms and their consequences, unintended as much as intended, were changing the Soviet Union in ways that were probably irreversible. In a metaphor which was horribly mixed but served to convey the idea, I described them as 'cosmetic [that is partial] but explosive'.

As a solvent of the old Soviet system Gorbachev was very much to be encouraged. He was also a fact of life we could only accept. His career, successful or otherwise, would be governed by an internal dynamic we in Britain could do little to influence. We should welcome his reforms and maintain close contact with him. But Soviet military power was also a fact; and, lacking hard evidence to the contrary, we should remain wary of Soviet foreign policy.

This was the tenor of the advice I gave the Prime Minister in minutes and frequent discussions. It accorded very much with her own ideas. She made the acute remark that Gorbachev was trying to make the system work better but failed to realize that the system itself was the problem. We should, however, welcome his reforms as a testimony to the failure of Communism.

She also wanted to build on her first contact with him. She had quickly summed him up as a man to do business with. We had had to expel a large number of Soviet agents in March 1985, one of those recurrent purges made necessary by the persistence of Soviet espionage. But, that done, she wanted to draw a line and get on with a constructive relationship. Here she was ahead of other Western leaders and she was naturally alive to the presentational advantage of showing that Britain enjoyed easy communication with both superpowers. Being close to Reagan added to her attractions in Moscow; and as the interpreter of Gorbachev she would be doubly welcome in Washington. I suggested a Moscow visit in 1986; but she was hesitant, fearing there might be too little to show. The plan was put off until 1987.

On the other aspect of the new regime, external policy, she remained very sceptical. The conclusion had to be that Soviet foreign policy had changed in style but not in substance. Unlike his predecessors, Gorbachev was innovative, restless, agile, a skilful propagandist. He and his advisers were producing a series of superficially attractive proposals on arms reduction which would go down well with Western governments unwilling to carry the burden of heavy defence expenditure and eager to believe the best of the new man in Moscow.

But the thrust of the proposals had not changed. Just as in the days of Brezhnev and Gromyko, they were designed to formalize or enlarge existing Soviet advantages, to block American development of SDI, or eliminate nuclear weapons. The advocacy was better, however; and by this approach, at Reykjavik in October 1986, Gorbachev came very near achieving a decisive shift in the European balance of power. He spoke eloquently about co-existence and might have been more sincere in his regard for the concept than his predecessors, for whom it was simply a term for varying the intensity of the East-West struggle. But the military facts remained: the weight of Soviet arms overhanging Western Europe; the modernization of missiles; the expenditure on research and development. In 1986, for example, among a variety of new military programmes, there were further deployments of a new mobile intercontinental missile (SS25). Another new type (SS24) was being tested. A new strategic bomber was going into production; and new cruise missiles were undergoing trials.[14]

The other touchstone was Soviet activity in the Third World. Though Gorbachev's remarks at the 27th Party Congress in 1986 suggested that support for 'wars of liberation' would no longer be a Soviet priority, there was no obvious slackening in Soviet activity in this area. In the same year very large new credits were extended to Nicaragua and Vietnam, and military assistance was given to Angola. There was a pro-Soviet coup in South Yemen and new, advanced weapons for Libya and Syria.[15]

In the face of these facts, no responsible Western government could afford to lower its guard or ascribe benign intentions to the Soviet side on the strength of new faces and a programme of internal reform.

In theory there should have been more visible change: an inefficient economy was supporting continuing high military spending; this could not continue indefinitely. We were looking for the point where the two lines on the graph, economic output and military budget, would cross. We were also looking for some sign of a change of heart, a faltering in the will to maintain the existing pattern of activities at whatever cost.

The test case proved to be Afghanistan. For the Soviet leaders the occupation was proving a costly and unpopular commitment, in Gorbachev's own words 'a bleeding wound'. The possibility of withdrawal had been in the air since he came to power: such a move would make economic sense and greatly improve his credentials in the West as an exponent of *détente*. But it would be very damaging in other contexts. Afghanistan was not a distant adventure, as in Africa or the Caribbean. It was a state bordering on the Soviet Union itself and its occupation was a major extension of Soviet power. It was the first time since the Second World War that Soviet forces had invaded a country outside the Soviet empire. Over 100,000 Soviet troops were committed there; and they had suffered heavy casualties. The enterprise could not be seen to fail. To withdraw would explode the Brezhnev doctrine on the irreversibility of Soviet gains and raise fundamental questions about Soviet determination to defend the empire elsewhere, particularly in Eastern Europe.

It was for these reasons that in Gorbachev's first years the analysts, and I include myself here, thought withdrawal on balance unlikely. The Joint Intelligence Committee had on the whole a good record of analysing and predicting the turbulent course of events in the Soviet Union in those days and later, even to the extent of foreseeing the ultimate collapse of the Union and the coup of 1991. But if the JIC is to be faulted it is on the grounds that we overestimated Moscow's determination to defend its territorial gains and its readiness in the last analysis to resort to force in that cause. So, we were not surprised that the Russians fought on in Afghanistan. If that was their intention our policy had to be to demonstrate that aggression had a high price. Together with the Americans we did what we could to help the mujaheddin.

But by the end of 1987 there were unmistakable signs of change. In February 1988 Gorbachev announced his intention to withdraw; the Americans seem to have been told some months earlier. Our object now became to ensure that the withdrawal was complete and that the Afghan government was not a puppet. But whatever the composition of the regime in Kabul, the withdrawal marked a watershed in Soviet policy and opened up a whole new range of possibilities.

By late 1988 the scene inside the Soviet Union was changing further and we were moving into the second and more dramatic stage of Gorbachev's reforms. The 1988 Law of State Enterprises tried to mix market freedoms with state planning; but the combination of enterprise autonomy with continued state control of prices proved disastrous. The old economy was being destroyed, but there was nothing to put in its place. Party resistance to the changes intensified; and at this point, in an attempt to seek a new and firmer political base, Gorbachev made his most dangerous move: he shifted the centre of political decision-making from Party to state. In March 1989 a Congress of Deputies, many popularly elected themselves, elected Gorbachev as President of the Soviet Union. A year later the same Congress repealed Article VI of the Constitution, which gave legal cover to the Party's leading role. The same constitutional changes provided for free elections in the republics. So that at one stroke the only effective power structure in the Union was disestablished; and at the same time the fissiparous non-Russian forces within it were given a stronger institutional base. From that point on, reform became political free-fall.

In his final years Gorbachev ruled in a dual capacity, as President via a Presidential Council and as General Secretary of the Party. Party and state organs were officially separated in July 1990. But the state, which had exercised power hitherto only as a façade for the Party, proved a very inadequate substitute. And the nationalist ferment, given further sanction by the constitutional reforms of 1989, was proving a fatal separatist force. There were civil wars in the south. The Baltic states demanded independence. Most serious of all, the Russian Federal Republic acquired a separate identity and Gorbachev's sworn opponent, Boris Yeltsin, became its leader.

Against this background of domestic ferment Soviet foreign policy remained remarkably effective. The goal was unchanged: a denuclearized Western Europe decoupled from the United States and increasingly vulnerable to Soviet pressure; but the packaging was much glossier and the customers more receptive. For many in the West, the Soviet threat was seen in a simplistic way, as meaning, are the Russians likely to attack Western Europe? Under Gorbachev this came to look implausible and the conclusion was that there was no longer anything to worry about. The fact that the

Soviet government could reach its goal by a combination of selective arms agreements and politico-military pressure was overlooked.

As his domestic troubles deepened and his domestic popularity fell sharply, abroad Gorbachev's stock rose. In the West he was acclaimed as a miracle-worker, the man of the year. He was awarded the Nobel Prize. Western leaders speculated anxiously on the solidity of his regime and asked themselves whether something could not be done to ensure his continuance in office. The consensus was that any successor must be less liberal. The Italian Prime Minister suggested a new Marshall Plan for the Soviet Union. And the German leader, Franz-Josef Strauss, visiting Moscow in the winter of 1988, declared that the Soviet Union had ceased to be a military threat to Western Europe.

Gorbachev skilfully exploited these openings. He began to talk of a 'common European home', where all states would be members of the same family and alliances would presumably be irrelevant. The trouble was that some members of the family remained rather better armed than others. His announcement in December 1988 of unilateral cuts in Soviet conventional forces still left disparities of 2:1 in the Soviet favour. He was pressing for the removal of short-range nuclear weapons and on his visit to London in April 1989 issued a sharp warning to NATO to drop plans for modernizing tactical nuclear weapons. This last seemed at the time a good example of the way we could expect Soviet influence to be exerted once we all got inside the walls of the common home.

Nevertheless there was no denying that his charm offensive worked well. The ideal prescription had been that a united and vigilant West would watch from a position of security the changes in the Soviet Union induced by its combined civil and military burdens. In fact the glue was failing in both alliances; the Germans were proving unreliable on nuclear weapons; the Danes had to hold an election on the issue of nuclear ship visits. Neither side was in full control of events.

The climate of Gorbachev chic affected even the strongest

spirits. The Prime Minister entertained no illusions on Soviet foreign policy. But she was becoming dangerously attached to Gorbachev in his domestic role. She admired his courage; she recognized a fellow reformer as well as a debating partner. Her visit to Moscow in the spring of 1987 had been an unqualified success, 'the most fascinating and invigorating visit I have ever made abroad as Prime Minister'. She had many hours of private conversation with Gorbachev, the Foreign Secretary not admitted. She mixed with the Moscow crowds; in a television broadcast, coached by Gordievsky, the former KGB agent who had defected to Britain two years before, she told her Soviet audience much about the international situation that had been withheld from them; and she devoured Soviet interviewers. In purely bilateral terms the visit did not accomplish much; but presentationally and on the wider stage, it was of immense value.

From then on, unfortunately, I found it harder to talk about Gorbachev with her entirely objectively. Her formidable powers of self-identification and advocacy were enlisted on his behalf. To me, in my jaundiced way, he was another Soviet leader, a remarkable one doubtless, who at home was doing sterling work in the Western interest, but one who was getting into ever deeper water and would probably not survive, one moreover who was concerned primarily with Soviet interests and would naturally be economical with the truth in their defence. My suggestions, and in the nature of things they became more frequent, that he might not be a permanent feature of the scene and that we should be thinking of life beyond him were coolly received. The Soviet leader, at least in his internal capacity, was becoming something of an icon.

I found this most sharply illustrated when I talked with the Prime Minister about Soviet chemical weapons. The Russians and their Warsaw Pact allies possessed very large stocks and there was hard evidence to prove it. But the Soviet government would admit to only a small amount, similar in quantity to that held by the United States. And Gorbachev specifically stated that his Warsaw Pact allies had never produced or stationed such weapons on their territory and that the Soviet Union had no chemical weapons outside its borders. These statements were contrary to the facts.

The Prime Minister, however, refused to admit the possibility that Gorbachev might be lying. She was sure that the facts had been kept from him. I said I thought this as likely as if, in a similar situation on our side, the facts had been kept from her. But she was hard to persuade. I found this worrying, not so much in this particular instance but rather as an example of a judgement that might now be flawed by personal sympathies. In the end, after some to-do, she tackled Gorbachev on the subject during his London visit of 1989.

13

The Soviet Union:
Collapse in Eastern Europe

THE RETREAT FROM Afghanistan had shown that, contrary to many predictions, the Soviet leadership were prepared in certain circumstances to accept the loss of socialism in an adjoining country. This raised profound questions about future Soviet behaviour and, as Gorbachev's reforms proceeded, those questions centred around the Soviet empire in Eastern Europe.

This was, as we hastened to remind ourselves, a very different proposition from Afghanistan. To the average Soviet citizen the war there was a costly misadventure. Dominion in Eastern Europe on the other hand was seen as the proper reward for the fearful expenditure of life in the Great Patriotic War. For the Soviet government it was also a glacis for the defence of the Soviet heartland; and it safeguarded communications with the crack Soviet divisions, some 300,000 men, stationed in East Germany. Defections from the Soviet camp in this part of the world could directly threaten Soviet security and were surely unthinkable. Nevertheless, Afghanistan posed the question: what was the extent of Soviet tolerance?

In East European countries, with their traditions of dissent and even revolt against Russian rule, Gorbachev's reforms naturally provoked ferment. Poland and Hungary, both leaders in non-conformity before Gorbachev's time, were again in the van. But

Gorbachev himself was circumspect in statements about the area. There was no attempt to export *perestroika*. It was clear where the master's sympathies lay; but the satellites were left to find their own level of liberalism. Gorbachev avoided laying down prescriptions and tried to improve consultation, or at least information, within the Council of Mutual Economic Assistance and the Warsaw Pact. As all Soviet leaders had done, he tried to get more out of Eastern Europe in terms of manufactured goods and food. Although his internal policies had set a dangerous example within the empire, he seemed in his first years almost exclusively concerned with reform in the Soviet Union itself.

By 1988 he was making more interesting statements in a general foreign policy context, saying that every country had the right to self-determination and, in a joint statement with his hosts on his trip to West Germany in June 1989, that all peoples and states were free to decide their destiny for themselves. These were revolutionary principles if applied to the East European satellites; but it was hard to believe that where Soviet security was concerned they were meant to be taken literally. As late as September 1989 the Soviet Foreign Minister, Eduard Shevardnadze, speaking at the United Nations, was qualifying them by emphasizing the need to respect 'post-war realities'.

On the Western side there was much caution and ambivalence. It was becoming clear that the Western economic and political system had won: Gorbachev was saying almost as much himself. But the West was uncertain how to exploit the advantage and keenly aware of how brittle the situation was becoming in Eastern Europe and, for that matter, in the Soviet Union itself. We wanted Gorbachev's reforms to continue; but we were uncertain how he, and we, would react if they threatened the Soviet empire and even the territorial integrity of the Soviet state.

From early 1988 we had been reporting the outbreak of ethnic conflict in the Caucasus, at first between Armenians and Azeris over the autonomous region of Nagorno-Karabakh, and then within Georgia. Unrest was visible in even more sensitive areas, Lithuania and Estonia. I recall talking to the Prime Minister at the end of 1988 about our response if the Baltic states were to revolt. We would of course speak out in their support. But in the end we both recognized we would probably have to acquiesce in Soviet suppression, as, unhappily, British governments had had to do in the past in the cases of East Germany, Hungary and Czechoslovakia. We had a deep interest in freedom in Eastern Europe, but an interest in stability which in the last analysis over-rode it.

The British government had hitherto pursued a selective policy towards Eastern Europe, treating each state on its merits and avoiding dealing with them through the Russians. We did our best to promote their commercial, cultural and political ties with the West. We encouraged economic reform and, more recently, political reform. As a prerequisite to it we held out conditional offers of economic aid. On her visit to Poland in November 1988, where she was given a rapturous popular reception, the Prime Minister had said in effect, 'Pursue political as well as economic reform and you will find the West more generous.'

In Hungary the local Communists had replaced their long-time leader, Kadar, and political opposition had been legalized. By 1989 there were therefore in Poland and in Hungary movements toward pluralism which we were sure we should applaud and eventually reward. But all this had to be done with much caution and with a wary eye on the great imponderable: what degree of change would Moscow tolerate?

I remember minuting the Prime Minister in early 1989 that we faced two big issues, how to hold the Western alliance together in the face of Gorbachev's seductions; and how to exploit the growing possibilities of change in Eastern Europe without provoking dangerous instability.

A proposal was floated at the time by some Americans (and it is a mark of our sense of both opportunity and danger that it was ever considered) to the effect that we might seek some arrangement with Gorbachev which would allow greater political and economic freedom for Eastern Europe against an assurance that there would be no military or security risks for the Soviet Union in this. The

East Europeans would remain members of the Warsaw Pact, but be given greater freedom within it.

I argued against this suggestion on the grounds that it would mean explicit recognition of the Soviet Union's East European dominion; that it would mean paying the Russians for something that was taking place in any event; and that if we came to face a crisis in some East European country we would find ourselves in an impossible position if we had in effect already accepted the Soviet right to maintain their military control.

The idea died, with few mourners, and both the Administration and we ourselves accepted that we had better keep our hands free, even if we could not foresee, and almost certainly could not control, the tide of events.

We still faced the question, how far could the East Europeans safely go? In Washington, on my visit in May 1989, we were talking about 'two impossibilities': losing the Party's leading role and leaving the Warsaw Pact, with the second as the less tolerable. But we shared a growing feeling that the longer *perestroika* went on, the harder it would be for the Russians to use force. We also worried that in his forthcoming meetings with Chancellor Kohl, Gorbachev might offer German reunification on condition of a neutralized Germany.

At that time my own hopes centred on Poland and Hungary, and in a talk I had with the Prime Minister in August I argued that Gorbachev's greatest gift to us could lie in Eastern Europe, more particularly in those two countries. His own prospects were clouded. But he still rode the tiger of reform and it was in our interest that he should continue to do so. He was apparently prepared to tolerate a degree of change, among Poles and Hungarians at least, which could have profound effects not only in Eastern Europe, but also perhaps in the Soviet Union itself. Our object should be, without gross interference, which would only backfire, to encourage that process to the point where it could become irreversible; in other words to establish facts, like a form of democracy and a free market economy in Poland and Hungary, which would have a chance of surviving the passing of

Gorbachev. If we could do that we would have accomplished a great deal.

Solidarity had triumphed in the Polish elections in June and Jaruzelski had accepted the results. The Prime Minister would need to remind Gorbachev when she saw him next in September that it was critical for his relations with the West that the Polish people should be allowed to pursue the reforms they wanted and that Polish Communists should co-operate in this. At the same time we would need to encourage the new Polish leaders to tread carefully in their relations with the Russians. Lech Walesa's assurances about adherence to the Warsaw Pact were wise. Thirdly, the West would need to review the question of economic assistance to Poland.

The Prime Minister agreed with the reasoning and undertook to speak in those terms to Gorbachev when she next saw him. But by September Poland and Hungary were overshadowed by a more important issue, Germany.

Looking at the East European situation earlier in the year, our analysts had not seen change in East Germany as imminent. Again, as in the case of Afghanistan, we overestimated the Russian will to hold on to their possessions. The East German security apparatus seemed to us still formidable. So it did to a variety of other observers. In the GDR, if anywhere, armed suppression of dissent, a European Tiananmen, was thinkable. And East Germany was central to Soviet security; for Moscow to abandon its position there would be tantamount to throwing in the whole hand.

The collapse in Eastern Europe, or, more accurately, the final act of the collapse, began in August. Hungary, which allowed almost all its citizens to travel to Austria, had an agreement with the GDR whereby East Germans trying to cross the Hungarian border illegally would be arrested and sent back home. In August the Hungarian government, possibly in return for West German credits, relaxed its controls on East Germans, who flooded through into the West, circumventing the Berlin Wall. By the end of September 40,000 had got through. When the East German authorities began forbidding travel to Hungary, the problem transferred itself to Czechoslovakia, with most of the emigrants finding refuge in the West German embassy in Prague. The mass exodus renewed queries about the legitimacy of the GDR regime and revived demands for internal reform.

By October there were demonstrations in Leipzig against the East German government. On 7 October, on his visit to East Berlin to celebrate the fortieth anniversary of the GDR, Gorbachev made it plain that he was not prepared to support Honecker in the latter's stand against reform. Soviet troops in East Germany were confined to their bases. Two days later, faced with a massive demonstration in Leipzig, the East German authorities recoiled from the use of force, though Honecker had apparently given orders for a 'Chinese solution'. Thereafter Communist rule in East Germany rapidly disintegrated. The Berlin Wall came down in November. By the end of the year, in a miraculous chain reaction, Communist regimes had disappeared throughout the former satellite orbit.

There remains even today an element of mystery in Gorbachev's acquiescence in this massive dismemberment of Soviet power. In theory he could have invoked the Brezhnev doctrine and forcibly suppressed East European discontents. But he would have personally found such a course repugnant, certainly more so than any of his predecessors. More important, he was already so far committed to another road, that of liberalization, that so savage a U-turn was probably impossible for him. On 25 October, on a visit to Helsinki, he said he had no right, moral or political, to interfere in the events of Eastern Europe.

But, if there was idealism, there was also major miscalculation. He seems to have believed that by liberalizing the empire he could retain it, that a reformed, more autonomous Eastern Europe would remain socialist and still cleave to the Soviet Union. Here we have another example of his persistent delusion that there was a middle way, that, for example, an improved and more open GDR could lead an independent life without falling into the arms of Federal Germany.

When he did realize the extent of his error it was of course too late. He had in any case become too dependent on Western goodwill for the success of his foreign policy and for the alleviation of his military burdens. His own public relations successes and the often naïve Western faith he had inspired combined to tie him down. Whatever he had meant when in 1986 he had redefined co-existence, he was now compelled to interpret it in the Western sense, as meaning interdependence and co-operation, no longer just a temporary relaxation in the eternal class struggle.

The year 1989 demonstrated in the most striking fashion Western victory in the Cold War. It did not, however, demonstrate Western unity. In particular it handed the leading alliance members a question which they had lived with comfortably enough for many years in its abstract form, but which they had not really expected to have to handle in practical terms and in short order, namely the reunification of Germany. After November 1989 the reunification question was no longer 'Whether', but 'At what speed?'

As she makes clear in her memoirs, the Prime Minister was moved and inspired by what had occurred, as she calls it, 'the most welcome political change of my lifetime'. I offered her for one of her speeches the lines from Shelley's 'Hellas', which Curzon had intoned in the House of Lords after the First World War:

> The world's great age begins anew,
> The golden years return,
> The earth doth like a snake renew
> Her winter weeds outworn:
> Heaven smiles, and faiths and empires gleam
> Like wrecks of a dissolving dream.

I am not sure that she ever used them, but they were appropriate.

At the same time she was acutely conscious of the fragility of the situation, as we all were. The victory was there; but it had to be con-solidated. Gorbachev might see military force as out of the question; but would he survive after such concessions? And would his successors think the same way? The Soviet divisions had not with-drawn.

The only prudent course seemed to be to take things steadily: first the internal liberalization of the GDR, free elections and the emergence of a state more nearly corresponding to its Western neighbours. Then, in due course, links with West Germany and ultimately reunification. In the meantime, no changes of frontiers; and the Warsaw Pact and NATO could exist as before. Gorbachev had insisted on continued Warsaw Pact membership when he and the Prime Minister met in Moscow in September. This did not seem an onerous condition: the Warsaw Pact was reassuring for him and at the same time highly permeable: it was no barrier to Western ideas.

Reasoning in this way, and at first she was far from isolated on the issue, the Prime Minister sketched out a stately progress towards reunification, a period of some ten to fifteen years. The trouble with this prudent scenario was that it did not take full account of the political pressures on Chancellor Kohl, the popular enthusiasm on either side of the Berlin Wall, and, above all, the sheer fragility of the East German state once the Wall was breached. In my minutes to her that winter of 1989 I pointed out that there was another scenario, marked 'Fast Forward'; and in the event it was this script that was followed, by actors who had no time to prepare their lines and who were equally in the grip of one of the great popular movements of our time.

East German Party leaders rose and fell in rapid succession: Honecker, Krenz, Gysi, each more frail and unmemorable than his predecessor. Once the Wall was down the mass exodus to the West resumed. The GDR economy proved so weak that monetary union between the two Germanies could not await the East German election planned for March 1990. And Chancellor Kohl, sensing an historic opportunity, took the bit between his teeth. He had issued his ten-point statement of 28 November for achieving German unity without consulting his allies. Now he decided on rapid incorporation of the GDR, more take-over than merger. He visited Moscow in February 1990, won Gorbachev's agreement to reunification, and on a later visit to the Soviet Union in July even extracted agreement to a unified Germany in NATO. The fact that large sums of German money, to cover Soviet troop costs, changed hands and that steady US pressure was throughout exerted in the same direction made it no less of an achievement.

It was in this period, particularly the early months of 1990, that, sadly, British policy went astray and we allowed ourselves to be seen as negative on German reunification. It was particularly sad in view of our firm public commitment going back some forty years to just that objective.

But the hard fact was that the Prime Minister did not like reunification; and this was visible to her staff from the opening of the crisis. To her it was an unpalatable irony that, after the expenditure of British blood and treasure in two world wars, we should be faced with a Germany able once again to dominate Europe. She had grown up during the second of those wars and for her, as for many of her contemporaries, the concept of Germany was indelibly marked by that experience. The fact that the German leader had a very different vision of Europe from her own, the integrated model rather than her '*Europe des patries*', made it worse. The final twist of the knife was that the American President, to whose attention she thought Britain had a particular claim, backed the German Chancellor throughout and added warm words about an integrated Europe.

To these more emotional considerations was added the reasonable fear that too rapid movement on reunification could bring Gorbachev down and provoke a Soviet backlash. I was in Moscow in February 1990 for talks with Chernyayev, Gorbachev's Foreign Policy Adviser, and Akhromeyev, his Military Adviser, and had direct experience of the depth of Soviet concerns. By then they were prepared to concede the principle of German reunification; but they were intent on getting the external framework right and as many ropes round Germany as possible. Here they saw the Prime Minister as an ally. They differed from us, however, on German membership of NATO. They saw logic in our case that a neutral Germany would be much more destabilizing, but asked how they could accept a situation where the principal restraint on Germany was the military grouping formed, as they saw it, to threaten them. They played strongly on the theme of adverse domestic reaction in the Soviet Union and the likely damage to Gorbachev. 'This is an additional burden he does not need' was the refrain.

The Prime Minister was not alone in thinking and feeling as she did. Other Western leaders shared her concerns. In two private meetings President Mitterrand was eloquent on the subject. The difference was that her partners composed their features and said very different things in public. The Prime Minister was all of a piece; she had little guile. What she said in public did not differ much from what she said in the most highly confidential discussions. And on Germany she allowed herself to speak out and be cast in the role of the nay-sayer. The fact that it was not all-out opposition, merely a plea for care and delay, mattered little: the press had the caricature they wanted.

Thus there was no great British gesture of support towards Germany on the issue of reunification. What was worse there was no recognition that this was a game we could not hope to control on our own: the key players, apart from the Russians, would be the Germans and the Americans, who saw things differently; we had no allies. The Prime Minister's attempt to turn President Mitterrand from the Franco-German axis and convert him into a fellow obstructionist on the reunification issue was foredoomed; it fatally underestimated the strength of the ties built up between Paris and Bonn and the considered French reaction that they would now have to get closer to Germany: if there was to be reunification, it would have to be balanced by the fact of a more integrated Europe. Against that background, our policy was a failure of calculation as well as imagination.

I found my own role trying during those months. Normally the Prime Minister and I looked at matters from a broadly similar standpoint. I was usually able to make an impact even where I could not persuade. In this instance we were apart.

My advice was that reunification was going to happen whether we liked it or not. Britain was publicly committed in its support. Whatever her private reservations might be, we should hasten to embrace publicly what we could not prevent. If we tried to swim against the stream we would merely sour our relations with our allies and reduce our influence, particularly in Washington. From the wider standpoint, what was happening was an immense victory for the West and for principles she had been foremost in advocating. It might not be an unalloyed pleasure for her. But it would be tragic if, because of this private qualification, we failed to be given the credit due and allowed ourselves to be edged away from the centre of influence in the new Europe that was emerging.

Later, the main object, as I saw it, was to get a reunified Germany into NATO and avoid the trap of reunification on terms of neutralization. As far as the Soviet Union was concerned, this was achieved by American pressure and German money, more specifically by President Bush at his summits with Gorbachev in December 1989 off Malta and in May 1990 in Washington, and by Chancellor Kohl in Moscow in February and Stavropol in July 1990. As far as the Prime Minister was concerned, assent to the proposition came at a meeting of ministers and officials at Chequers in January. This was the meeting personalized and immortalized in Alan Clark's diaries. He chooses to present it as a defence review based on a paper he submitted. But there many other papers; and what it was really about was getting the Prime Minister over the principle of reunification and on course with the issue of the moment, namely its terms.

The 'time of troubles' over Germany dragged on for the first part of the year. Negative statements (as in the Prime Minister's January interview with the *Wall Street Journal*) were balanced by more positive ones (as in her speech to the Board of Deputies of British Jews in February). The Foreign Office said the right things; but the cat was out of the bag and the damage done. The ill-effects were prolonged by the famous March seminar at Chequers on, of all things, the German character and the leak of its record. Fortunately, I was out of the country at the time. Then came Nicholas Ridley's comments to *The Spectator*, for which he had to resign, but which seemed to many only a cruder version of musings at No. 10.

There were occasional lighter moments. I recall an interview the Prime Minister gave an eminent Sovietologist who had come to talk to her about *perestroika*. Despite her German distractions, she kept her appetite for news about Russia. Or so it seemed at first. But as her visitor spoke, at some length, she nodded off. She had had a particularly tiring day and it was one of the few occasions I saw her show physical weakness. She awoke suddenly, her visitor still in full flow, and in her conscientious way decided he deserved her contribution on the subject. The trouble was that the only subject at that time as far as she was concerned was Germany. She spoke vigorously on that topic and her visitor left, bemused and shaken.

In the end the bulk of the rescue work on Germany was done by Foreign Office ministers and officials, who laboured with great skill and devotion together with their alliance colleagues in the Two plus Four negotiations, that is the two Germanies, plus the United States, the United Kingdom, France and the Soviet Union, the four powers with occupation rights dating from the Second World War. These talks settled the external aspects of reunification. The British contribution earned genuine German gratitude, as I saw when I visited Bonn in the summer of 1990. There all looked sunny again; and I was impressed by the confidence with which my hosts spoke of turning the East German economy round. Four to five years would be enough they said, though some were even more optimistic. Here, still low on the horizon, was the first cloud of another crisis, the cost of reunification and its impact on European economies.

14

The Soviet Union: The Last Act

From the military as well as the political standpoint the events of 1989 transformed the European scene, though with a rather greater time-lag. The Soviet armies were still in place; but they were pledged to withdraw from Hungary and Czechoslovakia in 1991; and before long they were also committed to withdraw from the eastern parts of Germany. Assessing the scene for the Chequers meeting in January 1990, I said there could be no assurance that Gorbachev would survive; nevertheless, a successor regime in Moscow, weakened and distracted by deepening internal problems, would almost certainly be unable to reverse the process of liberalization in Eastern Europe. Western Europe would still need a cohesive defence organization strengthened by a substantial American presence and by nuclear weapons; and for prudent defence planners the Soviet Union could be expected to remain the principal external threat for many years to come. But we were in a new world.

What was important now was to exploit the immense opportunities available and regularize the new situation on the basis of permanent Soviet troop withdrawals and a lasting balance of security. There was a coincidence of interest: Gorbachev was desperate for the savings only troop withdrawals and demobilization would bring; for Western leaders Soviet conventional superiority had always been the fundamental threat. Now there was scope for real improvement. In the new conditions the East-West negotiations for conventional force reductions, which had pursued their arcane and unproductive course in Vienna for many years, were jolted into life; and in November 1990 a Treaty on Conventional Forces in Europe (CFE) was signed in Paris. It cut down by almost 70 per cent the number of tanks, artillery pieces and armoured combat vehicles the Soviet Union could keep west of the Urals.

In the military and political manoeuvres of the time, which inevitably centred round German reunification, the US government acted with great skill, sensing the way the tide was running, and its speed, working in concert with Chancellor Kohl and thereby avoiding the danger of a bilateral Soviet-German bargain, which could have been on the basis of German neutrality, insisting on a reunified Germany remaining in NATO, but at the same time providing sufficient reassurance for Gorbachev to avoid Soviet acts of desperation. The Western performance was impressive; but it was one in which America and Germany held the leading roles. Britain, for all its expertise in the Two plus Four discussions, was in second or third place, and sometimes, it seemed, in danger of moving off the stage altogether.

Echoes of the Prime Minister's personal rearguard action against rapid reunification lingered some way into 1990; and on NATO strategy there were corresponding Anglo-US tensions. Mrs Thatcher felt that President Bush was going dangerously far in military gestures in his efforts to soothe and reassure Gorbachev and keep the Germans aboard.

The President was anxious to make the NATO summit of July 1990 a public relations success as a means of reconciling the Soviet government to the new order of things, in particular to the fact of Germany remaining in NATO, and also as a way of soothing German worries over nuclear weapons. In consequence he wanted to play down the nuclear component in NATO strategy. Early American drafts for the summit communiqué proposed a description of nuclear weapons as 'weapons of last resort'. The Prime Minister rightly objected that this undermined the strategy of flexible response and came near to accepting the Soviet proposition of 'no first use of nuclear weapons'. It also went further than the formula she thought had been agreed at her recent meeting with the President in Bermuda.

In the end there was some watering down and the NATO declaration was invaluable in helping Gorbachev overcome criticism at the July Communist Party Congress in Moscow. The episode was in some ways a replay of the strains over short-range weapons a year earlier. Britain was arguing along sound military lines; but we were out of tune with the political mood of our allies. We were once again in the position of 'anchor to windward', and this time, if anything, even further behind the fleet. These were not the best days of the Anglo-American alliance. We had to wait for the more direct military test of the Gulf War in August 1990 to remind Washington of its enduring virtues.

As we sought to consolidate the gains in Eastern Europe and, in so doing, banked heavily on Gorbachev's survival, we had to watch, with growing concern, the developing crisis within the Soviet Union itself. To be precise, there were several crises, running concurrently. There was first the rapid deterioration in the economy: the old system was disrupted but nothing effective was put in its place. Though many schemes were canvassed, Gorbachev was never prepared to cut the link with the old command-administrative system. His markets were always managed markets. By the end of 1989 the economy began to decline and a year later it was collapsing. At home Gorbachev was naturally held responsible for the distress and his popularity plummeted.

While economic reform stalled, political change accelerated. One of the strangest features of the scene was the disjunction between these two wings of the movement. Gorbachev took sweeping presidential powers in February 1990. But at the same time Article VI of the Constitution, guaranteeing the Party's leading role, was repealed. From now on he was having to rely on increasingly insecure political bases, living more and more on improvisations and tactical ruses.

In the autumn of 1990, in an attempt to guard himself against right-wing critics, he appointed KGB and military representatives to head the Interior Ministry. Yakovlev, his principal adviser,

1. A very, very special relationship:
Mrs Thatcher and President Reagan at Camp David, November 1986

2. Charm in the Kremlin: Mrs Thatcher and Mikhail Gorbachev
on her visit to Moscow, March 1987

3. Very friendly, but not quite as it used to be: Mrs Thatcher and President Bush at Camp David, November 1989

4. Not entirely at one on Europe: Mrs Thatcher and Sir Geoffrey Howe at the launch of the Conservative European manifesto, May 1989

5. Personal regard not reflected in policy: Mrs Thatcher and President Mitterrand in Paris, June 1988

6. The strains of reunification: Mrs Thatcher and Chancellor Kohl, March 1990

7. One unsmiling face: Mrs Thatcher at the European Community's Dublin Summit, June 1990

8. A fresh start in Europe? Mr Major and Chancellor Kohl at Maastricht, December 1991

9. The Gulf War Cabinet: (*clockwise*) Andrew Turnbull, Principal Private Secretary; Leonard Appleyard, Cabinet Deputy Secretary; author; Sir Robin Butler, Cabinet Secretary; the Prime Minister; Sir Charles Powell, Private Secretary; Gus O'Donnell, Press Secretary; Sir Patrick Mayhew, Attorney-General; John Wakeham, Energy Secretary and information co-ordinator; Douglas Hurd, Foreign Secretary; Tom King, Defence Secretary; Sir David Craig, Chief of Defence Staff

warned against an offensive by conservative and reactionary forces. Shevardnadze, his Foreign Minister, resigned in December with a dramatic prophecy of approaching dictatorship. More hard-liners were brought in: Pavlov as Prime Minister, Yanayev as Vice-President. Gorbachev may have believed he could control them and use them to moderate demands from democrats and separatists. But increasingly they came to look like his keepers rather than his adherents.

The third and most dangerous crisis was the revolt of the nationalities. Elections in the republics in early 1990 brought separatists into the lead in the Baltic states, Moldavia, Georgia, Armenia and the Western Ukraine. There were calls for sovereignty and bids for economic autarky. The republics refused to contribute to the Union. Most serious of all, as part of the same centrifugal process, the Russian Federation was acquiring an independent identity and falling under the influence of a bitter enemy. Yeltsin became Russia's parliamentary leader in May 1990 and its elected President in June 1991. Once in authority, he was ready to outbid Gorbachev on *perestroika*, economic reform and democracy. He was also prepared to champion the oppressed nationalities, less out of altruistic devotion to their cause than as part of the overall struggle for power.

Independence demands by nationalities and Gorbachev's rejection of force in Eastern Europe raised real possibilities of the break-up of the Soviet Union. From late 1989 onward the JIC came to see this as increasingly likely and the forecast was part of the assessment used at the Chequers meeting in January 1990. At first it seemed possible that a tougher line might be taken against disaffected republics than against the East European satellites: there were repeated attempts to browbeat the Baltic states and resorts to limited violence, usually in disavowable circumstances. But in the end the same restraints operated. The whole *perestroika* venture was posited on the avoidance of old-style repression. Nor by this stage could Western reactions be disregarded. President Bush was not prepared to jeopardize the whole US-Soviet relationship in support of the Balts; but at the Malta summit he was able to extract a promise from Gorbachev to avoid bloodshed.

As a result, Gorbachev's options narrowed and his credibility at home fell, as it rose abroad. Having installed the hard men and allowed them to use some force in Lithuania and Latvia, he had lost the support of many democrats and nationalists. By preventing the reactionaries from completing their work, he alienated the right as well.

Western governments watching this scene faced a series of questions, almost all unprecedented. They had to form some judgement of where events inside the Soviet Union were leading. They had to balance their investment in Gorbachev against thoughts of his growing vulnerability and against their instinctive support for the 'imprisoned people' of the Soviet Union, above all those in the Baltic states. They had to balance the immense gains already achieved in Central Europe, and the need to secure and fortify these, against the more doubtful prospects further east. Increasingly too, they were having to discuss the question of economic aid for the Soviet Union.

This last issue became active in the summer of 1990. I recall Teltschik, Chancellor Kohl's Foreign Policy Adviser, raising it with me in Bonn in June. He spoke of the need for very large sums, much more than Germany alone could bear, which would not only help preserve Gorbachev and orderly reform, but also help secure Soviet acquiescence in politico-military issues. Western advisers might be supplied to do something to ensure the money was sensibly used.

I said I sympathized with the wish to help. But there were serious objections. There was as yet no framework into which the money could usefully be injected. More advisers would not suffice; what was needed was something much more radical, something like a receivership of the Soviet economy. So far we lacked even the basic commitment on the Soviet side to market development. Without that, or much greater Western control, we would be pouring money into a black hole.

The question was considered by our principals at the G7 meeting of leading industrial countries at Houston in July. Kohl and Mitterrand argued for some $20 billion in aid. The Russians asked for three times as much over a period. The Prime Minister was very cautious, as was President Bush. Until the Soviet economy was restructured and Soviet military spending reduced, there could be no confidence that Western funds would be wisely used. There were in any case serious objections, particularly in Congress, to aid for the Soviet Union while the Baltic states were still under thrall and Soviet aid was still being used to back left-wing regimes in Angola and Cuba. But the unreformed state of the Soviet system was the clinching argument.

In the end Gorbachev had to be satisfied with offers of international studies of the Soviet economy as a prelude to possible Western aid. It was a negative answer; but I thought it was the right one. It was a realistic recognition of the limits to our capacity to influence the deteriorating Soviet internal situation. In the end it was probably wiser to use what Western money was available to help the new democracies in Eastern Europe. There we had something to build on and a much higher chance of success.

By the spring of 1991 massive repression by the centre directed against the Union republics was ceasing to be a practical proposition. The question was rather the degree of balance to be achieved between the two. And it was no longer a matter of concessions by Gorbachev to leading republics; the boot was on the other foot. Now it was a matter of how much of their gathering power the republics were prepared to pass to him to preserve at least the appearance of effective central institutions. The emergence of anti-Communist forces in the Russian Republic under a freely elected leader was the decisive development, leaving the Kremlin as little more than a husk. The critical issue became the terms of a Union treaty. Gorbachev had by now swung back to reform. He sought to conciliate Yeltsin and leaders of other republics and negotiated a treaty which would concede autonomous powers to the republics in a loose confederation.

It was this treaty, due to be signed on 20 August, which was the immediate cause of the coup of 1991. There had been a false start in June when, in Gorbachev's absence abroad, the Prime Minister, Pavlov, tried to have the presidential powers transferred to his own office. Now there was a more serious attempt.

For some time the JIC had been warning, not only of the coming disintegration of the Soviet Union, but also of the danger of a right-wing coup. They went on to say, however, that they doubted whether such a coup would hold and prove able to turn the clock back for long. These were prophetic words. Nevertheless, when the coup came in August it came out of a clear sky: there were none of the signs that normally precede an attempt of that kind, what I called the marks in the snow. But then, one reflected, the coup was led by professionals like Khryuchkov, the KGB Chairman; he, above all, would know how to cover his tracks. So it was a rather sombre gathering of the heads of the intelligence agencies that met in my room in the Cabinet Office on the afternoon of Monday, 19 August, the first day of the coup. We had to envisage a period of perhaps months before popular forces would be able to reassert themselves. But then the Assessments Staff, under Gordon Barrass and Gloria Craig, who had been in permanent session throughout the day, began to point out curious features of the situation. Gorbachev was incommunicado; we had expected no less. But Yeltsin was very visible. According to the normal laws of such operations he should have been eliminated in the first hour. But pictures of him were appearing on local television; he was alive; he was seen on a tank. Something very odd was happening.

The next morning I suggested to the Prime Minister (since November 1990 John Major) that we attempt to telephone Yeltsin. It was a long shot but worth trying. The Prime Minister had already issued a condemnation of the coup, the first by any Western head of government. That afternoon he telephoned Yeltsin, using the hot line installed after Mrs Thatcher's visit to Moscow in April 1987. He got through as if it was a local call. Yeltsin was delighted to be contacted and by the message of support, to which full publicity was given. He gave a dramatic account of his situation in the White House; he expected an attack that evening. That accorded with our own intelligence. But, as we now know, army leaders met to discuss the crisis in Moscow that evening and decided against action. Gorbachev's *perestroika*, whatever its failures, had so far changed Soviet society that the strong-arm methods of the past no longer came automatically.

The coup collapsed the next day. The plotters' behaviour throughout was marked by irresolution, confusion and inefficiency. One of them, it appears, was drunk throughout. The absence of indicators for us to read beforehand, it now turned out, was not because of professionalism but sheer lack of preparation.

Gorbachev returned from captivity in the Crimea to what he called a changed country. It was more changed than he knew. Extraordinarily, he still defended the Communist Party and spoke of its renewal. But its rule was over. On 23 August the Russian Parliament suspended its activities and sealed its headquarters. In Moscow joyful crowds defaced or destroyed the statues of its founding fathers. The removal from outside the Lubianka of the giant statue of Dzerzhinsky, the first head of the Communist secret police, had a special symbolism.

The time for a Union treaty, however liberal, was also gone. Yeltsin, intent on removing the last niche for his rival, was determined to bring the Union to an end and did so on 8 December when, in agreement with the leaders of Ukraine and Belorussia, he proclaimed the Commonwealth of Independent States. Gorbachev finally left the Kremlin on 25 December.

The Joint Intelligence Committee is an austere body. It rarely rejoices and it lives too close to the dark side of political activity, the plots, revolutions, defections and betrayals, to find much ground for surprise, let alone celebration, in the events it analyses. But the proscription of the Soviet Communist Party, which had been the prime object of its study for so many years, was memorable even against that bleak background. After our meeting of 29 August I asked the Committee to join me for a glass of champagne. We drank to the demise of the Party and added a toast to the plotters of 19 August who, in the best Marxist fashion, had given a push to history. For whatever the coup failed to accomplish, there was no doubt that it had wonderfully foreshortened events. As Yakovlev himself later said to James Baker, 'They did for us in three days what would have taken us fifteen years to accomplish.'[16]

15

Europe:
Same Bed, Different Dreams

WHEN THE FOUNDER members of the Common Market met at
Messina in June 1955 for the conference which resulted in the
Treaty of Rome, they invited the British government to join them in
their work. Britain sent to the Spaak Committee that autumn, not a
minister but an official, an Under-Secretary from the Board of Trade,
who was instructed to call himself a 'Representative', not a 'Delegate'
like the others. He left before the Spaak Report was finalized and is
reported to have bowed out with dismissive words about the whole
Messina enterprise. In style the version usually given shows signs of
having been improved by some later, probably French, hand; but its
substance clearly accorded with British government thinking at the
time and it is therefore worth quoting, even in that form:

> The future treaty which you are discussing has no chance of being
> agreed; if it was agreed, it would have no chance of being ratified;
> and if it were ratified, it would have no chance of being applied.
> And if it was applied, it would be totally unacceptable to Britain.
> You speak of agriculture which we don't like, of power over
> customs, which we take exception to, and of institutions which
> frighten us. *Monsieur le président, messieurs, au revoir et bonne chance.*[17]

That statement would serve as an epigraph for almost any
account of British relations with Europe since the Second World

War. The story is to an alarming extent one of mistaken assessments and missed opportunities. Britain regularly overestimated her power and as regularly underestimated the strength of the impulse, particularly the political drive, behind the European grouping. The result has been a depressing chronicle of delayed awakening to reality, of belated arrival in institutions fashioned by others, of repinings, second and third thoughts, divided counsels and qualified enthusiasms, and a general confusion of policy which still afflicts us and seems designed to achieve maximum pain and minimum influence.

By chance, I saw a little of policy on Europe in my earliest days in the Foreign Office when, as a very junior member of the Economic Relations Department, I was able to sit in on the official committees which considered our approach to the Common Market. They were impressive gatherings, clever, self-confident men who were sure they had the measure of the European visionaries. They were dominated by the Treasury and thought almost exclusively in economic terms. Like their colleague from the Board of Trade, and like the ministers to whom they reported, they doubted whether Messina would come to anything; and they were sure that, if it did, they could checkmate it with the British plan for a European Free Trade Area. We have seen the outcome.

These are of course the vanities and miscalculations of the distant past; but they are perhaps a not inappropriate preface for some comments on what was the most turbulent and controversial aspect of foreign policy in Mrs Thatcher's time.

The comments are, unfortunately, less personal and informed than I would like, and less so than those elsewhere in this book, for the simple reason that I was less active in this sector of policy than any other in the theoretically unlimited brief I held as Foreign Policy Adviser. The Community figured of course in the regular reviews of the international scene that I prepared for the Prime Minister as a basis for talks with her; and bilateral relations with France and Germany came under the spotlight from time to time. But policy toward the Community as a subject for advice proved elusive, being either highly technical and the province of the dedicated experts in the Cabinet Office, or so explosive as to be tackled by the Prime Minister only in private, and reluctant, meetings with senior colleagues, such as those over the European Monetary System in the summer of 1989. Europe, it soon became apparent, was a nerve issue; but perhaps because of that it lay below the surface and was rarely if ever exposed. There were no large strategic discussions, no seminars. And by the time the latent Cabinet divisions emerged, in Mrs Thatcher's last three years, there was no room for persuasion. The lines were drawn and it was a matter of executing rather than debating policy, and executing her policy at that.

As regards contacts in European capitals, with Horst Teltschik, Chancellor Kohl's adviser, and Jacques Attali, his French equivalent, Charles Powell, as Private Secretary, saw much more of them than I did. He was also present at some London meetings, for example on the Delors report on monetary union, which I did not attend.

My own initial attitude to the Community was much influenced by the fact that it was not a unified force able to operate on the outside world in the politico-military issues of the time in the way that the United States, or individual European governments, or even NATO could. And those issues, whether in East-West or Middle East relations, were immediate. As an international actor, the Community was *in posse* not *in esse*. This was also a factor in the Prime Minister's attitude. As regards the Community's future, I was less sceptical than she was, or became. I could not, and still cannot, see a plausible future for the United Kingdom outside Europe; and I remained much more doubtful than she was of our capacity to stop the clock in European integration and establish as a final destination a co-operating group of independent nation states. It was a simple matter of putting oneself in the other side's shoes and understanding what drove them on. I also took a different view on German reunification and the best place for a reunified Germany in Europe. But these differences did not emerge until relatively late in the day; and by then minds were closed.

Looking back, it is perhaps natural to assume that the Thatcher years were a period of uninterrupted hostilities with Europe, a kind of Napoleonic War, broken only by the occasional Peace of Amiens. In fact it was not like that. There were perhaps three stages. The first was dominated by the continuing battles over the Community budget, which had begun with her first government in 1979 and were not concluded until Fontainebleau in June 1984. The second, from 1984 to say 1987, was a much more positive period, in which Britain pressed for the completion of the single market and took a leading part in drawing up the Single European Act. The third, and darkest, phase covered Mrs Thatcher's last two years in power. It was marked by disputes with Europe and divisions within the government itself; and its characteristic expressions were the Delors report on monetary union on the one side and the Bruges speech of September 1988 on the other.

In her days as a member of the Heath government the Prime Minister must have paid routine obeisance to the European idea; and we know she campaigned strongly for Europe in the referendum of 1975. But it is difficult to see her as ever having been a true believer. Certainly, throughout the period I knew her, her private attitude to Europe ranged from suspicion to undisguised hostility. She did not like the Europeans; she did not speak their languages; and she had little time for their traditions. She recoiled from the Eurojargon, as who did not; and what she saw as the Continental penchant for grand generalizations offended her lawyer's mind.

Europe was therefore pre-eminently an area of struggle, an arena. The patronage from Giscard d'Estaing and Helmut Schmidt that she had to endure when a new girl at the summits of the early 1980s is often adduced as the cause of her antagonism. That may have had something to do with it, but not very much; the roots went deeper. Moreover, the arguments over money, British money, her money, which were the theme of her first five years, lent themselves easily to a confrontational approach and to her concept of foreign affairs as a series of separate battles from each of which she had to emerge as victor.

She had of course a very strong case. Because of the nature of its trade and agriculture, Britain contributed much more to the Community budget than British economic performance justified.

We received relatively little from the Community agricultural funds, but provided a substantial part of the Community's tax revenue. After Germany, we were the Community's biggest paymaster; almost all our other partners were significant net beneficiaries.

Though the case was clear, it was not easy to translate into equitable solutions and fair rebates. And there is little doubt that without intransigent and on occasion, as it seemed, outrageous behaviour on the Prime Minister's part, we would not have succeeded. Her tactics were sound, and effective at home as well as abroad: the theme of Britain facing down the Brussels bureaucrats and recovering British money played well in the constituencies.

But there were costs. Our European partners did not enjoy the experience and were in consequence less responsive on later issues, in most of which Britain stood to gain by a measure of co-operation rather than flat vetoes. Perhaps the heaviest costs were borne by the Prime Minister herself, in character deformation, in the confirmation of her prejudices, her suspicion of the Foreign Office, by whom she may not always have been well advised in the early budget battles, and in her growing conviction that the tough approach was the only one that would pay dividends with the Europeans and secure British interests.

With the Fontainebleau settlement behind it, the government was able to adopt a much more positive attitude to the Community; in fact the years from 1984 to 1987 could be regarded as our *communautaire* period. We wanted to take part in European construction, if only in one well-defined area. Attention was concentrated on completing the single market, on removing non-tariff barriers and creating a Europe that was frontier-free for goods, services and capital. From this, it was reasonably calculated, Britain stood to gain a great deal.

Within the Community much of the impetus behind a true common market had faded once internal tariff barriers had been lifted and a common external tariff established. But the legal obligation to complete a single market remained in the original Treaty of Rome; it was a matter of reviving and implementing it in full with a reasonable deadline: 1992 was fixed on. The practical question was how to bring our partners to accept this target without having to pay an extortionate price.

The eventual bargain, for, like all Community achievements, it was an elaborate compromise, was enshrined in the Single European Act agreed at Luxembourg in December 1985. It was the first revision of the Treaty of Rome. We had not wanted such a formal change, or the hazards of an intergovernmental conference which had to precede it. It was originally hoped that the decisions could be taken at Council level, in Milan in June 1985. But the Italian Prime Minister, as President, thought otherwise and Britain was outvoted.

As we had wished, the Act called for the completion of the market by 1992. In order to facilitate this, among its major provisions was agreement that on virtually all economic matters, apart from taxation, qualified majority voting would replace the old unanimity rule. This dropping of the veto was judged necessary if the market was to be completed in the limited time available and in the face of strong protectionist instincts on the part of most Community members.

This was almost certainly right; but it meant leaving the safe, and to Britain particularly attractive, ground of veto-power. We took comfort in the fact that the Luxembourg compromise was unaffected (the convention whereby a member state retains a veto where a very important national interest is at stake); though it is arguable that the Luxembourg compromise now has no significant part to play in Community business.

The gains were clear; but a price had to be paid. The shift from unanimity raised the issue of how far Britain would be prepared to accept majority voting on proposed extensions of the scope or application of Community law in, for example, matters of immigration, health, or conditions of employment. Having unlocked the gates in the areas where we wanted progress, we could not be surprised if others with differing ideas of the Community's ultimate form sought to exploit the new freedom for their own purposes. At Luxembourg nothing was given away in these sectors; but they would be areas of renewed struggle in the future.

The main debit entry, however, lay in the inclusion in the Single European Act of references to economic and monetary union. The Act itself had a chapter providing (harmlessly) for closer economic and monetary co-operation in Europe, but entitled (more dangerously) 'Co-operation in Economic and Monetary Policy (Economic and Monetary Union)'.

These references were themselves a compromise, only a watered-down version of more full-blooded proposals from M. Delors, the Commission President, and his supporters. Nevertheless they represented a concession, a beachhead which the integrationists and those seeking monetary and eventually political union were able to expand enormously in the next few years.

Was the price excessive? It can be argued that it was a strategic error to include any such wording, however qualified. But against the background of earlier repeated declarations by the Community in favour of economic and monetary union and the immense political pressure in that direction from most of our partners, it is very doubtful whether a total omission would have been within reach. Given a choice between a static and a dynamic Community, there was no doubt which would prevail. And in such a gathering, progress on exclusively British terms was not practical politics.

What was becoming more apparent, moreover, was a fundamental clash between the Prime Minister's Gaullist conception of a *'Europe des patries'*, members of a single market but independent and sovereign, and the more dynamic, integrationist, political vision of her European colleagues. This in turn raised the question of British policy if, as seemed only too likely, British blocking tactics proved ineffective and Community development took forms we could not approve. The issues which still divide Britain and divide Britain from Europe were already discernible.

This external clash was complicated by growing divisions between the Prime Minister and her ministerial colleagues on the tactics to adopt in handling it and the nature of the ultimate relationship between Britain and Europe. The Foreign Secretary Geoffrey Howe and the Chancellor of the Exchequer Nigel Lawson were both alarmed at the Prime Minister's increasingly strident and adversarial style in Community councils. They saw this as too often counter-productive, uniting Europe against us and denying ourselves the opportunity of influencing developments and promoting British interests by flexibility, by skilful use of *communautaire* language, by exploiting differences, by swimming with the stream rather than always against it. The Foreign Secretary went further and was prepared to envisage Britain's membership of a less static Europe and even, on suitable terms, of a monetary union. Both, originally on domestic grounds, favoured early British membership of the Exchange Rate Mechanism (ERM) of the European Monetary System (EMS), which, since 1979, Britain had been committed to join 'when the time was ripe'.

The Prime Minister, with her eye firmly fixed on what she was coming to see as a basic Euro-British contradiction, dismissed these fears and the proposed compromises as Foreign Office defeatism. She did not despair of us getting our way and in any case saw intrinsic merit, and, increasingly, domestic gain, in fighting the Continental powers and the Brussels bureaucrats. As regards the EMS, she did not see it as a valuable anti-inflationary tool. She wished to retain her freedom of economic and financial manoeuvre; and in any event, she was determined to have the final word in matters of high policy. As she put it in a memorable interview with the Chancellor, 'I must prevail.'

Some of these divisions emerged earlier than others. The first, fruitless, attempts at persuasion over EMS took place in 1985; then the matter was put away and lay like a well-acknowledged skeleton in the Downing Street cupboard for some years – perhaps the one issue on which, if it were raised in Cabinet, the Prime Minister would have found herself in a minority.

Unfortunately during those years Europe did not, probably could not, stand still. The case for monetary union was developed and a committee of central bank governors, under the chairmanship of Jacques Delors, was commissioned to present a report to the Madrid European Council in June 1989. M. Delors, proclaiming his faith in the growing strength of the Community to the European Parliament in July 1988, forecast that in ten years' time eighty per cent of economic legislation, perhaps even fiscal and social as well, would be enacted by an embryo European government. For the Prime Minister this was inflammatory talk. The effect was not improved by M. Delors' appearance at the TUC Conference at Brighton to loud applause from a socialist audience.

The contradictions between Britain and Europe were now presenting themselves ever more sharply to Mrs Thatcher; and they were reflected in her speeches. Her address to the College of Europe at Bruges in September 1988 has a special value as a milestone in her progression to more explicitly anti-European attitudes. It was drafted for her by Charles Powell, was much revised by the Foreign Office, then to some degree restored by the speaker and her secretary before delivery. I saw only the earlier drafts. It was a curious speech in that the substance was not markedly heterodox. But the tone and imagery, and the presentation by her Press Secretary, revealed strong Eurosceptic tendencies; and it was by the rhetoric and presentation rather than the content that it was, correctly, judged by its audience.

The same anti-European tone marked the government campaign in the June 1989 elections to the European Parliament: 'Do you want a diet of Brussels?' It was not a successful campaign: there were substantial Conservative losses. But it illustrated what was by now a curious dichotomy in British policy. At working level Britain was pursuing the old, reserved but generally pragmatic approach to Europe, which would allow for a co-operative, if unenthusiastic, relationship for many years to come. At the top, however, there was a much shriller, chauvinist note, which presaged a direct clash. In fact it could be said that two distinct lines were being pursued, one by the Prime Minister, one by the Foreign Secretary. This was a situation that could not last. In the Prime Minister's household it was easier in such times to be the executant or spokesman for her line, like Charles Powell or Bernard Ingham, than to be her adviser, particularly when the adviser did not see entirely eye to eye with her. But at this time and on this issue dissenting advice was wasted.

Meanwhile the Delors report had emerged and presented Britain with painful tactical decisions. The report was in three linked stages. Stage 1 provided for the completion of the single market, closer European monetary co-ordination, the development of the ecu and entry into the EMS by all Community members. Stages 2 and 3 laid down subsequent moves to the ultimate union. A particularly dangerous paragraph (39) stipulated that a decision to embark on Stage 1 was equivalent to a decision to embark on the entire process.

It was on this paragraph that British eyes fastened. A rearguard action was inevitable and its object had to be to undo paragraph 39 and detach Stage 1 from Stages 2 and 3, in other words, as usual in British plans on Europe, to allow for limited conformity. But in order to reach this goal and prevent treaty amendments which would apply the whole report at once, Britain had to display some respect for Stage 1 and undertake to join the ERM very shortly, rather than finding repeated excuses for not joining, as the Prime Minister continued to do.

This was the background to the celebrated joint *démarche*, or, more strictly, *démarches*, for there were two, by the Foreign Secretary and the Chancellor to the Prime Minister on the eve of the Madrid summit. The two ministers saw this as an overdue discussion on the need to join the ERM, a move they had long advocated as a piece of financial and economic good management and now pressed on the further, tactical, ground that it would divert the Community from the wholesale adoption of the Delors report. The Prime Minister saw it in a very different light, as a conspiracy, an attempt to blackmail her with threats of resignation into a supine and *communautaire* course, when she felt it necessary to keep her options open. In essence, she saw it as a threat to her authority.

Surprisingly, her statement at Madrid was much as her petitioners had asked, quiet, conformist, with a reaffirmation of Britain's intention to join the ERM, subject to certain not very onerous conditions. It was also sufficient to take the trick: Stage 1 of the Delors report was adopted; Stages 2 and 3 were left for further study. The Prime Minister had come close to accepting the recommendation of her ministers. But it was at a heavy cost in resentment, which led within months to the Foreign Secretary's dismissal.

In his account of these events in his memoirs, Geoffrey Howe cites as an example of the Prime Minister's isolation the fact that, while her senior colleagues had to adopt extraordinary measures to extract an interview with her on a critical issue within their responsibilities, she was ready to hold a meeting of all her No. 10 advisers to discuss the same topic in depth at the same time. I am afraid he exaggerates the extent to which advice on the Community was sought in those days. The meeting, which I attended, was brief and superficial, more a review of accepted positions than a genuine examination of the choices before us. But it is true that the Madrid episode, when a ministerial request for consultation could be construed as conspiracy, illustrated an alarming breakdown of communication and trust within the government.

I recall sending the Prime Minister a short minute before Madrid, emphasizing the strategic importance of ensuring that Britain was not marginalized in Europe. This would mean that we would be seriously diminished in the eyes of major powers like the United States and Japan. Of course we would have to judge carefully the cost of staying at the centre. But we should not rush to the conclusion that the cost would be excessive, or underestimate the importance our partners attached to carrying us with them. It was worth a real effort to show that our position was not entirely negative. What this meant in practical terms at the coming meeting was an early volunteered statement in as flexible terms as possible about our intention to join the ERM.

I have no illusion that this counsel had any impact. In the climate of the time, how could it? But it is worth recalling as an illustration of how our problems appeared to one interested observer.

The Madrid summit was in its curious way, and at immense internal cost, a success for Britain. But it was tactical and temporary only. The pressure for monetary union grew; its adherents, checked at Madrid, prevailed at succeeding councils, and at Rome in October 1990 it was agreed that Stage 2 would begin in 1994. This meant another treaty revision. There were also proposals for political union. The British rearguard action was becoming increasingly arduous and its casualties multiplying: the Foreign Secretary fell and, in falling, helped bring down his leader; the Chancellor too lost his post, though this had more to do with economic management, and economic advisers, than with the Community. The Prime Minister's dominance, and isolation, grew ever more pronounced. Belatedly, Britain joined the ERM. But the Prime Minister's personal comments on Europe grew more unyielding: she made it clear that, whatever the official formula, for her a single currency was out of the question.

When she lost power herself in November 1990, in part as a result of Conservative concern over her handling of Europe, the questions that were to dominate the next few years were clear. Would the drive to European integration succeed? How was the relationship between an integrationist Europe and a nonconformist Britain to be managed? If our future lay in Europe, what price were we prepared to pay in order to retain our position and our influence there? What alternative futures were there for a detached or semi-detached Britain?

The Prime Minister's answer to these conundrums had proved increasingly simplistic, a retreat from the demanding game of wheeling and dealing in the Community to a stark assertion of national sovereignty, a *ne plus ultra* approach. As she put it in her comments in the House of Commons after the Rome summit: 'We have surrendered enough.' This prescription raised many hard questions about Britain's future place in the world. But it had emotional appeal, not only for her, but also for many in the country, worried or puzzled by Community developments and for long lacking any positive government guidance on the European case. Euroscepticism was becoming a force.

To complete these impressions of European policy during Mrs Thatcher's last five years, I should say something about bilateral relations with France and Germany. Against the background of Community debates, in which tactical alliances with this or that partner were the order of the day, there were sporadic efforts on our part to raise relations with Paris or Bonn to a new level. The object was to balance the Franco-German axis, always the main force in Community politics, to alter the balance of power in our favour, or simply to prevent Britain from being marginalized.

These efforts were not very successful, though they led to interesting encounters and exchanges. France was attractive as a possible partner. The Prime Minister liked and even respected President Mitterrand. Despite his socialist principles, he took a hard view of the Soviet Union. He also found her personally interesting: '*Les yeux de Caligule et la bouche de Marilyn Monroe.*' In the Community France and Britain had some common ground. Both were intensely nationalistic, relying on the Council of Ministers, distrusting the European Parliament. And as nuclear powers, they should have been natural allies. But when it came down to any detail there were always snags.

On the nuclear side, it was our close links with Washington. Another major obstacle was the French desire to build up Europe as a force independent of and, it seemed at times, hostile to the United States. In the world at large we found ourselves, naturally and instinctively, siding with Washington, while the French insisted on a prickly, independent position.

In Europe, nothing could shake the French determination to assert political and intellectual leadership with the economic support of Germany, a leadership best realized through the control of Community institutions and Community policy. And in the pursuit of that objective nothing could outweigh the German connection. After German reunification the French became even more intent on keeping close to Bonn and accelerating European integration. Between London and Paris there seemed always an underlying clash of national interest. Britain had arrived too late, or could not bid high enough. Perhaps it all went back to that distant day in November 1956, when the British halted their invasion of Egypt and Adenauer told the French Prime Minister, Guy Mollet, 'Europe will be your revenge.'

Germany seemed in some ways an easier proposition. We were both close allies of the United States, both net contributors to the Community. From time to time I would argue the importance of getting closer to the Germans in the context of NATO, or East-West relations, or the Community. The Prime Minister would agree; and the best resolutions would be made. But they came to nothing. Mrs Thatcher underestimated Herr Kohl and there was no natural sympathy. She responded coolly to his genuine attempts to establish a rapport. She did not take to the food on her visit to his home village of Deidesheim. But there were more solid grounds. She thought him, and even more his Foreign Minister, Herr Genscher, unreliable on nuclear weapons, and perhaps on East-West relations generally. She was jealous of the attention President Bush gave him. She was at odds with his integrationist aims in Europe and his wish to strengthen the European Parliament. To this was added the trauma of German reunification.

Here she employed a curious argument. When I urged that Germany, if as dangerous as she alleged, would be best managed within the European Community, she replied that the only effect would be to give Germany a larger unit to dominate and control. It seemed that she saw less danger in a Germany without any restraints, operating in a Europe akin to that of the 1930s. I did not find this at all convincing. It seemed to me that the French, as usual, were being more logical. Ideally, they sought to run Europe, drawing on the economic resources of an obedient Germany. When it became apparent that this dream was unrealizable, and that German economic strength would confer superior political muscle, they still saw advantage in having a hold on the Bundesbank via a seat on a European central bank, rather than letting a united Germany roam free, with the Bundesbank still in practice able to dictate French interest rates.

16

Europe: Maastricht and After

WITH MARGARET THATCHER'S fall some of the fever went out of the air on Community issues. European leaders were very ready to ascribe many of their problems with Britain to personalities; and John Major in any case wanted a less high-pitched debate.

In minutes to him I was able to say, without too great a sense of unreality, that Britain's future lay in Europe and that we could not afford to be marginalized. In a speech in Bonn in March 1991 he expressed the same thought: 'I want us to be where we belong. At the very heart of Europe. Working with our partners in building the future.'

His vision of Europe remained one of co-operating nation states, with strong Atlantic ties and a recognition that NATO would continue to provide basic European security. Development had to be by evolution, not rushed or forced. On monetary union, Britain reserved judgement. In substance the message was not so remote from Mrs Thatcher's at Bruges. But the tone was very different.

As a new man, without an awkward European past, he was able to repair relations with Germany and build up a personal understanding with Chancellor Kohl, which stood him in good stead at Maastricht. As part of this process, I recall a series of tête-à-tête lunches I had with the German Ambassador, in which we went over our positions in some detail. There was a fair measure of agreement and much goodwill.

At home the Prime Minister was untroubled, for a time at least, by Cabinet divisions on the issue. Discussion on Europe at ministerial level became unusually open and harmonious, a genuine consultation. Some of the accumulated Downing Street power flowed back to the Foreign Office; Douglas Hurd gained in authority and became a very senior and supportive colleague.

But the underlying problems were unchanged, those of a reluctant Britain facing an impatient Europe. How to respond to pressure from Community partners for major advances toward a single currency and, a more recent addition, toward political union? How to remain in the council chamber and retain maximum influence without giving vital positions away?

The vital positions were first, freedom of action over monetary union. The proposed treaty changes would mean acceptance of Stages 2 and 3 of the Delors report. Stage 2 might be acceptable for us, provided adhesion was not taken as acceptance of Stage 3 at the same time. Stage 3 had to be made subject to strict preconditions to ensure a real convergence of economies before the final step was taken; and there must be freedom to opt in or out.

Second, freedom from the Social Chapter. The rest of the Community wanted such a section in the treaty on political union. This would mean that Britain, having freed its own labour markets, would be compelled to accept some at least of the higher social costs obtaining on the Continent and with that a loss of competitive power.

Third, from the British point of view it was essential that increased co-operation in foreign policy and defence, which would be at the heart of the coming treaty on political union, should be co-operation between national governments, rather than within the institutions of the Community, with the Commission in the driving seat and the results under the jurisdiction of the European Court. An alternative route for European development had to be found. In architectural terms, European construction would allow for separate pillars, foreign and defence. Similar reasoning applied to interior and justice matters. Also to immigration, which Chancellor Kohl wanted to bring under Community control; though for good tactical reasons it was decided to fight the battle of the frontiers away from Maastricht.

On the substance of defence, NATO, which alone assured the vital American military presence in Europe, had to remain the principal European security organ. New defence structures that would undermine NATO's role were to be avoided. On foreign policy, Britain was ready to co-operate and would seek as much common ground and concerted action as possible, but would not compromise the right to take its own decisions when national interests were at stake.

Greater powers could be granted to the European Parliament so as to increase its control over the Commission; but final power of decision in Europe must rest with the Council of Ministers, that is with national governments. Provision must be made to restrict Community action to those areas where it made more sense than national or regional action; the vague concept of subsidiarity had to be given legal force.

These were the main objectives. Unusually, and dangerously, it was decided to set them out in the Commons in November 1991. It was a curious fact that the provisions of Maastricht, both before and after the final summit, were examined and debated more rigorously in London, the doubtful partner, than in any other Community capital.

What was also remarkable was that at Maastricht virtually all of the objectives were achieved. Britain's right to decide whether or not to join a single currency was enshrined in legally binding form. The Social Chapter was taken out of the treaty and given a separate protocol, signed by eleven member countries only. It was agreed that European co-operation over foreign affairs, defence and law and order would intensify, but on an intergovernmental rather than a Community basis. Defence arrangements preserved the primacy of NATO. On foreign policy, unanimous voting would be necessary to authorize joint action, though detailed action within that framework could be taken on a majority vote. The European Parliament was given a limited role in monitoring the Commission. Subsidiarity had a clause in the treaty and a mention in the preamble. For good measure, Britain helped secure a commitment to the enlargement of the Community, covering negotiations for the entry of European Free Trade Area countries and later the former Communist countries of Central Europe.

Given the government's brief, it is difficult to see what more could have been done; it was a remarkable achievement; and a certain triumphalism in its presentation to Parliament in December 1991 could be excused.

But if the treaty, with its opt-outs and its pillars, was a success for Britain, it was also one for the Community. Notable advances had been made toward the 'ever closer union among the peoples of Europe' set out in the original Treaty of Rome. Treaty provisions for a rapid transition, under tight economic discipline, to economic and monetary union, with a single currency and a central bank, would have seemed visionary only a few years earlier. The treaty on European union was wider in scope than earlier treaties and brought in new policy areas. Progress by co-operation outside Community competence was now an acknowledged alternative route forward, but some members would continue pressing for a United States of Europe within one institutional framework. The question of a European defence identity was far from settled. A new intergovernmental conference to determine the Community's future and to review sectors such as foreign policy and defence was envisaged for 1996. Set against this prospect, the Prime Minister's claim of 'Game, set and match' was premature or even misleading.

From the British point of view Maastricht was a considerable success. But it was a success in a prolonged rearguard action. It allowed us to remain at the table with a voice on future plans. It kept some of our options open. But it did not prevent further advances by the Community in a direction many in Britain, and particularly in the Conservative Party, did not want, advances which posed sharper choices for the country on its long-term relationship with Europe. The Maastricht terms bought some time; but this was at the expense of a greater impatience with British negativism among European governments and a growing Euroscepticism at home. In the end Britain was left with no clear strategy; and significant sections of its politically active classes acquired a stake in dangerously negative developments on the Continent, in the hope of the collapse of monetary union and the failure of the European venture.

Seen in retrospect, Maastricht was perhaps the high point for moderate pro-Europeanism on the British side, just as it was the high point of linear progression for the Community. After Maastricht the mirror cracked and the issue of Europe became clouded and fissured by new doubts and problems both in Britain and on the Continent. Many of these were becoming apparent even before I left Downing Street in June 1992.

The first reminder that all was not well with European unity at the popular level came in June 1992, when the Danes rejected the Maastricht Treaty in their first referendum. In some ways more revealing and damaging was the wafer-thin majority for the treaty in the French referendum later that year. The European governing élites remained firmly *communautaire* and pushed on with their plans, but it was becoming apparent that some of them at least were markedly out of touch with their electorates. In the jargon of the Community, there was a growing democratic deficit. This alienation was part of the wider disillusionment with government which observers and politicians were encountering throughout the West.

Even at government level all was not as it should have been. After Maastricht the Franco-German axis, though still powerful, was not quite the irresistible force that it had been. In Germany doubts grew on the advisability of replacing the mark with an untried single currency. Over time it also became apparent that a substantial number of Community countries would be unable to satisfy the strict criteria laid down at Maastricht for making the plunge into a monetary union at the first opportunity. The prospect of a two- or three-speed Europe, or one with a variable geometry, became more plausible. It was even conceivable that the strongest powers themselves might find monetary union in 1999 an unattainable goal, a bridge too far.

If the mood among the believers was uncertain, how much more was this true in Britain, the home of European disaffection.

Europe and the Community had always had a greater domestic impact in Britain than any other branch of foreign policy. For many years the issue had divided the Labour Party. Now the virus, in new and more virulent form, began to attack the Conservative Party, the original party of Europe. A principal carrier was the former Prime Minister herself. Her attitude had become progressively more anti-European in her last years in office. Out of office fewer constraints operated and before very long she was the acknowledged centre of Euroscepticism, the high priestess of a heretical but increasingly influential sect. Her adherents, many of them former ministers in her cabinets, strengthened and sharpened the core of anti-European Conservatives who had survived from the early debates on British entry in the 1970s.

Her relations with her successor as Prime Minister were delicate and variable. There were differences of view. There were also well publicized reconciliations and expressions of support and solidarity. She said John Major had done 'brilliantly' at Maastricht. But she later explained that that did not mean that she approved of the outcome. In any case, the reunions were too frequent to be convincing. And the settled, though undeclared, attitude on her part was probably one of dissatisfaction with the European, as most other, policies of the men who had displaced and succeeded her in 1990. Criticism over Europe became an important means of conveying her dissatisfaction with subsequent events and a general unwillingness to come to terms with recent history.

A fundamental tenet of the Eurosceptic doctrine was that Britain should reject European monetary union, or anything beyond a community of co-operating sovereign states. To this were added, at various times and according to individual tastes, calls for the renegotiation of this or that aspect of existing Community arrangements, or for the repatriation of powers. Many of the proposed revisions would in practice amount to British withdrawal from the whole European undertaking; and there was much confusion and wishful thinking about the terms Britain could expect in such eventualities.

Events and accidents gave momentum to the Eurosceptic

current. In September 1992 Britain was forced to beat an ignomin-
ious retreat from the Exchange Rate Mechanism of the European
Monetary System. The government's credibility was severely
dented and the European cause suffered in the process. Nor was
the parliamentary arithmetic helpful. Thatcherite landslides were
things of the past. After April 1992 John Major had a comfortable
working majority; but one which could not afford a group of
twenty to thirty malcontents plotting within it. The Maastricht
Treaty was acclaimed in the Commons immediately after signature;
but its passage through the new House in the form of the
European Communities (Amendment) Bill became a prolonged
travail and humiliation; and ratification was only achieved in July
1993 after it was made an issue of confidence in the government.

Throughout this time reporting and comment in the British
press were steadily and sometimes virulently anti-European. The
insular case was always easier to present, with simple appeals to
British sovereignty, historical glories and traditional institutions.
Europe was something distant, threatening, technical, involving
foreigners, obscure regulations and hard choices. Neither from the
press nor the government was there any positive case for the
Community. For ministers and public, Europe remained a case of
last resort rather than first choice.

There was also much wishful thinking about the more sceptical
popular mood on the Continent after Maastricht. This was readily
interpreted as a wholesale conversion to British attitudes. 'Europe
is singing our tune now,' the Foreign Secretary said. The Prime
Minister wrote of the European commitment to economic and
monetary union as a mantra, as quaint and ineffectual as a rain
dance. Once again there was a failure to understand the determination of our European partners to push on.

Faced with these domestic trials, the Prime Minister's instinct
was to accommodate rather than confront. He saw his first duty as
holding his party together. Since the Eurosceptics were much the
more assertive wing, the inevitable result was a slide of British
European policy to the right and its subordination to the requirements of party management. The paramount need to keep the

party united was evident as early as the Maastricht deal; and its urgency and compulsion grew with time. For a moment in 1991 it had seemed as though Britain could achieve a workable relationship 'at the heart of Europe'. But within a year or so the phrase had acquired an ironic ring. European policy had become the prisoner of domestic faction.

17

South Africa: A Second Chance

IN THE PERIOD covered by this memoir, South Africa proved to be one of those rare cases in international affairs, a story with an unexpectedly happy ending. Within a few years, an immense and, as it seemed, inevitable tragedy was averted, a political compromise was negotiated, transferring power from white minority to black majority, and a second chance was conferred, not only on South Africa itself but also, in consequence, on the southern half of the African continent. British policy on the South African issue was singular and controversial. The part it played in the great transformation requires assessment. On narrower grounds too, the subject is interesting as a prime example of Mrs Thatcher's style in foreign policy, and of the tensions between the Prime Minister and the Foreign Secretary in its execution.

When I was head of the Foreign Office Planning Staff in the late 1960s, we produced for the edification of ministers a map of the world on what might be called the planners' projection, that is with the countries magnified or reduced in size according to the extent of British interests. I recall how South Africa bulked large against a shrunken African continent.

Nor was this a misleading picture in the 1980s. South Africa was by far the most important military and economic power in Africa. It was a major British trading partner, receiving over £1,000 million worth of our exports in 1984. The United Kingdom was its principal single source of foreign investment. The country was strategically as well as economically important to us. It commanded the sea routes between the Indian and Atlantic Oceans and it had therefore to remain outside the Soviet sphere of influence. It was also the principal non-Soviet source of a number of strategic minerals.

There were closer ties. A considerable portion of the white South African population were of British extraction; and it was estimated that there might be 800,000 South African citizens eligible to hold British passports and having the right of abode in Britain if there were to be a breakdown of order in their own country. The domestic trouble factor was therefore high. In its modern form South Africa was in fact a British as well as an Afrikaner creation. As the former colonial power, we carried historical responsibility. As the leading Commonwealth power, we were still credited with a pivotal role. The South African political system stirred deep emotions in Britain as well as abroad. It was not an issue we could avoid, even if the Prime Minister had wanted to.

There was also a considerable legacy from past controversies and decisions. It was never a choice between comprehensive sanctions and no sanctions. Under decisions taken either at the United Nations or with the Commonwealth or at European Community meetings, Britain already banned the sale of arms, paramilitary equipment and oil to South Africa, restricted sporting contacts, and discouraged scientific or cultural collaboration. Individual British firms were already deciding whether or not to disinvest. The issue was what, if any, further steps should be taken by the government?

Nor was there any question that apartheid was an entirely reprehensible and repugnant system. In his memoirs, Geoffrey Howe seems to suggest that Mrs Thatcher lacked a real sense of the human suffering and humiliation it involved. But in fact her condemnation was throughout unqualified and sincere. What was at issue within Britain and between Britain and Commonwealth partners was the most effective means for the removal of apartheid. Was the work best done by maintaining contact with the South African government, or by ostracism and more sanctions?

The consistent answer from Mrs Thatcher and her ministers

from 1979 onwards was that constructive engagement was necessary. As Geoffrey Howe put it in October 1985, 'Nothing could be less constructive than disengagement in the present state in South Africa.'

This was a natural enough position to adopt, given traditional Conservative sympathies for white minority regimes in southern Africa. It was also unlikely that the Prime Minister would wish to draw back from that part of the world, following her striking success in Rhodesia at the beginning of her term. But the policy was also supported by an array of cogent intellectual arguments.

There was first the almost certain effect of mandatory economic sanctions on the South African government. There was little doubt that such measures would merely confirm the South Africans' sense of isolation and lonely virtue and stiffen their resistance to change. Of all people, Afrikaners were the least likely to respond satisfactorily to external pressure.

Not only would sanctions be counter-productive politically, they would be impossible to administer and police efficiently. The evasion of sanctions would become a profitable industry. These were not abstract arguments; they were based on sad experience. Britain had recent memories of sanctions against Ian Smith's Rhodesia. In fact, historically, sanctions had proved a singularly ineffective instrument of policy. As Robin Renwick, who was to be a highly successful British ambassador to South Africa, had observed in a book on the subject in 1981, recourse to sanctions should never be based on the fallacy that it is possible to deter aggression or otherwise change fundamentally the political conduct of states by the threat of economic penalties alone.[18] This was a fair judgement. Sanctions were a favourite means of expressing international indignation and they no doubt left a sense of achievement and well-being in the minds of those who voted for them. They could punish and, if sufficiently supported, they could weaken. But the examples of oppressive governments brought down or obnoxious policies reversed as a result of their application were rare indeed.

In fact South Africa presented only another example of that

recurrent foreign policy problem, how to deal with morally repugnant regimes. To the idealist, the academic commentator, the newspaper columnist, the answer in these cases is blindingly clear. For the practitioner, the minister with decisions to take, particularly for those with responsibility for exports and employment, the choices are not quite so easy: unappealing regimes are distressingly common in the world and cannot be ignored by a country like Britain with widespread responsibilities and trading interests.

In practice, Britain, whether under Conservative or Labour administrations, has found that, if our interests are to be protected and promoted, we have to take a broad view. Communication has rarely been cut off and constructive engagement at one level or another has usually been practised. This was certainly so in the case of the Soviet Union, which probably deserved President Reagan's characterization as the 'evil empire'. It was also true of China, despite its record over human rights. It had to be asked: what was different about South Africa?

The case for sanctions was also vulnerable if examined from the point of view of the South African people. Embargoes and disinvestment would reduce employment; and the poor, the black population, would suffer first. A stagnating economy would damage neighbouring countries, for whom South Africa was the economic engine of the region. Conversely, industry, business and the growing employment of blacks in the towns was breaking down apartheid and exposing its inner contradictions. It was no paradox that South African big business was in the forefront of reform. According to the Oppenheimer thesis (named after the former Chairman of the Anglo-American Corporation), apartheid survived on low economic growth; a growth rate of over 5 per cent would increasingly draw in blacks as skilled workers and would confer economic power and, by extension, eventually political power.

More severe sanctions would also reduce employment in Britain. Precisely how many jobs would be lost was much disputed. But there would certainly be injury; and there was the interesting testimony of Ted Rowlands, as a Foreign Office minister of the preceding Labour government, as recently as December 1978, to the effect that cutting economic links with South Africa could have 'severe repercussions on the domestic economy'.

Stricter sanctions would therefore do widespread harm; and, far from relaxing, would only intensify internal South African tensions. Indeed the African National Congress explicitly advocated such measures on these grounds as a weapon in the armed struggle they saw as inevitable.

For these reasons, the British government could not accept the pro-sanctions case. It also refused to see the South African situation as frozen and hopeless. It discerned movement toward a more liberal regime even under President Botha, for example the abolition of the Mixed Marriages Act and the grant of freehold and leasehold rights to blacks. What was important was to acknowledge such changes and urge more. The kind of measures to be taken by Britain should be of the positive sort, by education and training awards designed to develop a more skilled black labour force and by laying down codes of conduct for UK firms doing business in South Africa. There should be close and persuasive contact with the South African government. With the other main party to the struggle, the African National Congress (ANC), there could be no ministerial dealings, since it was an organization espousing violence; but at official level regular contact was maintained.

These were the principal arguments. I agreed with them and elaborated them. But it had to be recognized that we were not in an academic debating chamber and that logic was not always the decisive factor.

For one thing, Britain was almost alone in approaching the issue in this way. Chancellor Kohl was helpful but preferred to let Margaret Thatcher take the lead. President Reagan was also for constructive engagement. But Congress was not; and in 1986 he had to give way to Congress: his veto was overridden. On the other side were the massed ranks of Africa and the Commonwealth; and not just the new Commonwealth, but Canada and Australia as well, all convinced that further means of pressurizing President Botha had to be adopted and that such measures would eventually prevail.

These were not lightweight opponents. British interests in black Africa as a whole roughly matched those in South Africa; and while the Commonwealth was an intangible that Mrs Thatcher was not disposed to overvalue, threats to its unity such as those presented by the dispute over apartheid were not to be disregarded.

There was an even more serious problem, namely that the South African government did not always oblige by playing the part assigned to it in our strategy. Even at Chequers, President Botha could be blunt and unresponsive. The fact of such a visit was sufficient for him. But we needed at least the promise, and preferably the evidence, of specific liberalizing measures. Nor was the general direction of South African policy steady. From time to time, in the face of black unrest, or perceived external interference, Pretoria moved the other way, stepping up repressive measures, proclaiming emergencies, shooting rioters, or launching raids on neighbouring states. The period 1984 to 1987 was particularly difficult: there were two states of emergency, the first from July 1985 until March 1986, the second imposed in June 1986 and lasting until 1990; and international concern and pressure for more sanctions were in consequence at their highest. As I regularly reminded the Prime Minister, we were engaged in buying time. But the underlying assumption of that policy, namely that time was on our side, often looked hazardous.

In this exposed position, with superior arguments but a shortage of allies, facing regular challenge at the biennial meetings of Commonwealth Heads of Government and more frequently in EC Councils, we needed all the tact and dexterity we could muster. We needed lowest-common-denominator agreements with our Commonwealth or European partners, achieved in conditions of minimum friction. But at this point the differences in style between No. 10 and the Foreign Office became apparent. There was no division on objectives, though Margaret Thatcher in her memoirs unfairly claims that the Foreign Office wanted to sell out South to black Africa. It was simply a matter of how to play the summit meetings while retaining our freedom of action and avoiding damage to our interests.

The Foreign Secretary's instinct was to reduce friction as far as possible and maximize the sense, or illusion, of solidarity. In presentation he would have played up the small concessions Britain made at the Nassau Commonwealth summit in October 1985 and praised all for the unity achieved. The Prime Minister, on the other hand, was determined to show that her concessions at Nassau had been minuscule; she claimed she had moved only 'a tiny little bit'. This way of putting it only stored up trouble. But she was unperturbed at being in a minority of one. In fact such a situation was to her a proof of virtue; the sharper the confrontation, the more likely she was right. She enjoyed putting her case in the most provocative form and exploring the inconsistencies and hypocrisies on the other side. What about black African states who traded with South Africa while clamouring for sanctions? On a later occasion, what about Canada's rising imports from South Africa? And so on. It was good, knockabout stuff; but, strictly considered, it was an indulgence.

The Nassau meeting published a communiqué, an accord along standard lines, criticizing apartheid and South African aggression against neighbouring states, calling on the South African government to abandon apartheid, release Nelson Mandela and start an internal dialogue, reaffirming the sanctions already in operation and making some small additions. It also agreed that a group of eminent Commonwealth persons, led by General Obasanjo, former head of the government of Nigeria, and Malcolm Fraser, former Liberal Prime Minister of Australia, should visit South Africa to forward the aims of the accord. Moreover, it was stipulated that if no progress was made by the group, a mini-summit would convene in August to consider further steps, including cutting air links with South Africa and banning agricultural imports.

This was ambitious. Given the internal condition of South Africa and the small likelihood of major improvement, it was probably over-ambitious. We were buying time at a high price.

The visit began well: in March 1986 President Botha lifted the state of emergency and announced a number of liberal measures. But two months later, the scene suddenly changed. The South

African armed forces launched raids against what they claimed were ANC bases in Zambia, Zimbabwe and Botswana. The genesis of the order for this operation was, and still is, obscure. But the opposing policies of March and May revealed the two sides of P.W. Botha's divided soul. A new and more rigorous state of emergency was proclaimed in June; the eminent persons hastily abandoned their visit; and the contingent undertakings of further measures made the year before were now invoked.

At this juncture Mrs Thatcher produced another temporizing device: she would dispatch Sir Geoffrey Howe, in his capacity as President of the European Community Foreign Ministers' Council, on another mission to South Africa to explore whether, despite the failure of the eminent persons' group, some progress in the direction of reform might not still be made. In the circumstances, in the aftermath of the South African raids and the eminent persons' discomfiture, the idea had more than a touch of desperation; and the Foreign Secretary, as the appointed victim, felt it more than most. Nor were his prospects of rewarding dialogue with African leaders improved by briefings from No. 10 emphasizing the Prime Minister's determination to give no ground on sanctions (though ministers had approved a more flexible line).

This was, as the press said, 'punch-bag diplomacy'. But the Foreign Secretary went through the ordeal manfully, was harangued by Mugabe and Kaunda, and endured two bad-tempered meetings with President Botha. Nothing was achieved and on his return, inevitably, further sanctions were agreed at the review conference in London in August. Other Commonwealth countries applied the measures they had held in reserve since Nassau. Britain was able to adopt a less swingeing package by accepting the more modest steps agreed on a contingency basis with Community prime ministers at The Hague in June.

In the rearguard action in which Britain was engaged over South Africa this had not been a particularly successful encounter. Admittedly, we had been let down by President Botha's tergiversations. But we had overestimated his capacity to deliver major reforms and had bought little time at the cost of rising

Commonwealth friction and the public humiliation of the Foreign Secretary.

In his memoirs Geoffrey Howe argues that these necessarily delicate manoeuvres were made even less manageable by the Prime Minister's contentious style and dislike of compromise. There is some force in his argument. There were of course marked differences in temperament between Prime Minister and Foreign Secretary. There was also an inevitable gap between foreign policy articulated by Bernard Ingham for the home market ('Maggie to make no concessions to blacks') and that expounded by the Foreign Office for the ears of Commonwealth and Community partners. But behind these variations in style and character lay more serious problems, as the Foreign Secretary was coming to discern, in the growing dominance of No. 10 and the diminishing trust between the Prime Minister and at least one of her senior colleagues. Britain's troubles stemmed only in part from South Africa; they were also home-grown, flowing from the fact of a divided command.

The years 1986–9, following the collapse of the eminent persons' mission, were arid and painful ones for South Africa and, in consequence, for British diplomacy dealing with the international repercussions of the crisis. P.W. Botha had begun as a modernizing president and was never wholly opposed to change. We now know that over a long period he maintained secret contacts with Nelson Mandela. He was also aware of, and countenanced, clandestine meetings between ANC leaders and Afrikaner establishment figures. But he relied too much on military advisers; he had no clear view of his goal; and he was by now incapable of the quantum leap the country needed.

South Africa lay under a state of emergency; the security forces were powerful enough to neutralize the main anti-apartheid organizations inside the country; the exiles of the ANC were unable to mount a significant guerrilla campaign from abroad. On the other hand, black leaders refused negotiation with the government on any terms less than the release of Mandela and his imprisoned colleagues, the legalization of the ANC, and an end to the state of emergency. Politically there was stalemate, a condition which played into the hands of those calling for severer sanctions.

The South African economy was in a dire condition. Foreign banks refused to renew credit. Foreign investment dried up. Foreign companies established in the country withdrew. What was worse, in 1986 the US Congress overruled President Reagan's veto and imposed sanctions. This added seriously to the economic pressure and left Britain politically more exposed.

Against this background, the biennial Commonwealth battles followed their predictable course. On the South African issue they had come to resemble a seasonal pageant play, with stock characters, set speeches and only limited bearing on reality, namely the situation inside South Africa. In the casting for these dramas Mrs Thatcher was automatically assigned the villain's role, a part she played, or overplayed, with relish. There was certainly strain on the Commonwealth and a concern that the roles of the Queen as the British monarch and the Head of the Commonwealth were being brought into conflict. But the danger of a Commonwealth break up on the apartheid issue was probably never great, though there was always much sound and fury.

At the 1987 Vancouver meeting the rift between Britain and her partners deepened. This time there were two press conferences. But there were no further sanctions and crises in Fiji and Sri Lanka diverted some of the pressure. The British argued for increased help for front-line states as a better use of Commonwealth energies than further punitive measures against Pretoria; a sensible argument, but one which did not go down very well.

At the 1989 summit in Malaysia the British delegation wrote their own communiqué; but the draft approved by the new Foreign Secretary, John Major, was too weak for the Prime Minister's taste. She composed her own rather less compromising statement.

By the time of the Kuala Lumpur meeting, however, dramatic changes were occurring in the only place that mattered, South Africa itself. In January 1989 President Botha suffered a stroke and was succeeded as President in September of that year by F.W. de Klerk.

On the face of it, de Klerk was an unlikely reformer. He came from stock as conservative as Botha's: his father, grandfather and great-grandfather had all been prominent Nationalist politicians and he himself was Nationalist Party leader in the Transvaal. In Botha's cabinet he had been a right-winger: he had supported racial segregation in labour and opposed trades union rights for blacks; he was uninvolved in any of the secret contacts with black leaders. But he was a pragmatist, a realist, and one who was prepared to revise his thinking in the light of an evolving situation. His brother spoke of him as undergoing 'an evolutionary conversion'. Like that other great reformer, Gorbachev, he began as a proponent of only limited reform; he at first rejected popular democracy and stood by group rights. But, unlike Gorbachev, he was prepared to follow the logic of the argument and abandon impossible half-way houses.

The impulses behind his conversion were various and have to be seen against the background of a widening recognition within South African ruling groups of the need for serious change. Ever since the breakdown of Verwoerd's 'Grand Apartheid', the impossible vision of total racial separation, white thinking had become increasingly fluid. Not only industrialists but also establishment figures like de Lange, the head of the Broederbond, the secret society of leading Afrikaners which had first devised the apartheid strategy, conceded that it could not survive and that the modern problem was how to retain white control without it.

The external environment was also changing and becoming less threatening. Under US encouragement, South African troops were withdrawing from Angola, as were Cuban forces; and Namibia was moving towards independence under United Nations supervision. Southern Africa, in common with other parts of the globe, was ceasing to be an arena for US-Soviet surrogate wars. Changes in Soviet foreign policy were removing the spectre of Soviet backing for the black anti-apartheid struggle; and inside the Soviet Union Gorbachev's reforms were offering a heartening example of radical change within a closed political system.

But the main sources of de Klerk's conversion lay nearer home, in his religious convictions, in his commitment to civil, as opposed

to military, government, in his awareness of South Africa's isolation, its serious financial crisis and, above all, the sterility of
apartheid. It was clear, to him at least, that things could not go on as
they had. Even so, it required great resources of intelligence,
courage and vision to act decisively, to break out of the Nationalist
laager, and to pursue the process of political transition to the end.
Against the background from which he emerged, he was an extraordinary and providential phenomenon. Mandela was, of course,
the other essential part of the South African happy ending; but in
some ways he was less remarkable than de Klerk.

The de Klerk *deus ex machina* transformed the arguments over
apartheid. The British strategy was vindicated. Beleaguered British
delegations in international gatherings saw relief at hand. The news
of the release of Walter Sisulu and five other ANC life prisoners,
one of the first steps in the thaw, was telegraphed by de Klerk to
Mrs Thatcher just before the Commonwealth conference in Kuala
Lumpur in October 1989. It enabled her to argue for the need to
reward progress and encourage further such moves rather than
persist with the philosophy of punishment. At the least, 'Give de
Klerk more time' was now a persuasive slogan. As he fulfilled his
promises, as Mandela was released and the ban on the ANC lifted,
Britain took the lead in undoing restrictions already imposed and
urging other governments to follow suit. Happily, the UN resolution of 1989 related the lifting of sanctions to signs of 'irreversible
progress' towards the end of apartheid, rather than the actual
transfer of power to the black majority.

The new situation also offered openings to British diplomacy in
Pretoria, which Robin Renwick skilfully exploited. Even in Botha's
days, the British position gave special access and leverage. After the
American sanctions of 1986 Britain provided the only effective
channel to the outside world. But Botha was refractory material.
With de Klerk there was scope for genuine dialogue about the
tactics of reform and for British steps over sanctions which could
be cited by de Klerk as evidence that liberalization was being recognized and having its impact outside the country.

Britain was also able to apply positive influence on another aspect of the South African crisis, namely regional relations. The Rhodesian settlement had done something to reduce the conflicts on South Africa's borders; but at the beginning of the period covered in this commentary the country was embattled. Its armed forces were heavily engaged in Angola, where there had been substantial Soviet and Cuban intervention since 1975. Namibia was under direct South African rule. ANC guerrilla fighters were established in bases around South Africa's borders and from time to time were the target of South African raids. The situation only deepened Pretoria's sense of isolation and persecution and encouraged regressive domestic policies.

On these issues London and Washington worked very closely together. We were fortunate in the realistic and vigorous policy pursued by Chester Crocker, President Reagan's Assistant Secretary for African affairs. The United States accepted the logic of constructive engagement and was ideally placed to exploit the opportunities offered by Gorbachev's new thinking, the Cuban wish to find an honourable exit from Angola, and the growing South African sense of being in a cul-de-sac.

The US-negotiated settlement of December 1988 gave Namibia independence under UN auspices and ensured the withdrawal of South African forces from Namibia and Angola and the withdrawal of Cuban troops from Angola. Britain played a strong supporting role, to which Crocker pays generous tribute in his book, *High Noon in Southern Africa*. We provided the main channel to the Angolans (there was no American diplomatic presence in Luanda) and were able to keep Western lines open in Pretoria. By good fortune, Mrs Thatcher was present in Namibia in April 1989, when the settlement was threatened by large-scale violations by SWAPO (the South-West Africa People's Organization); and her intervention rapidly restored order.

We were also active in encouraging better relations between South Africa and its northern neighbour, Mozambique. The British government provided substantial aid to President Machel and his successor, President Chissano, helping to wean them away from the Soviet orbit. And when the South African-sponsored RENAMO guerrilla movement (Mozambique National Resistance) seemed to be gaining favour in Washington, we were able to supply the Americans with damning evidence of the destruction it was causing in Mozambique. We saw training and support for the security forces of Mozambique, Zimbabwe, Botswana and Malawi as a sensible use of resources and as part of our constructive, as opposed to punitive, policy in the region.

How much in the end were we able to achieve; and what credit can we claim for the turn-around in the South African situation? Intellectually, our analysis was sound and was vindicated by events. The sanctions crusade was a self-indulgence, a policy of gestures likely to appeal to domestic emotions rather than make a serious contribution to easing the strains in the region. Indeed its immediate object was to heighten those tensions. British condemnation of that policy and practice of constructive engagement kept lines open to Pretoria when there was a danger of complete isolation and enabled the Prime Minister to exert steady pressure on the South African government for movement in a liberal direction. She could persuade and even threaten, as in her correspondence with President Botha, of which the implicit theme was that the position could not be held unless the South African government undertook further reforms. Once the new course had been set under de Klerk, we were able to bring greater influence to bear, as well as to assist in the rapid dismantling of sanctions.

In sum, Britain was able to do more than any of the other external actors in securing sane policies in South Africa. As Mandela publicly acknowledged when Margaret Thatcher visited the country after her resignation, 'We have a good deal to thank her for.' But external pressures, whether from Washington or London, were not decisive. The crucial factor was the emergence of an enlightened and courageous South African leader. This was our good fortune and not a necessary event: the old order could have held for several more years. Inevitably too, given the unyielding nature of South African attitudes and the level of international concern, much of the time was spent in dealing with the South African issue at second hand, in Commonwealth or

Community conclaves. In the first at least, the debates had at times an artificial quality and could almost certainly have been conducted at a lower level of friction. We performed well over South Africa; but we were lucky. Our contribution was unique, but its effect should not be exaggerated.

18

The Middle East:
Old Feuds, New Terrors

IN THE 1970s and 1980s, I suppose the majority of diplomats and analysts would have named the Middle East as the most dangerous area in a dangerous world, the place where, despite the prevailing superpower caution, wars regularly broke out, threatening to drag in the major players, where intractable regional disputes, the high level of armaments, and the presence of the world's main oil reserves, ensured that the stakes and the tensions were consistently high.

In 1984, when this commentary begins, the area fully justified such a judgement. In addition to the underlying Arab-Israeli dispute, that almost incurable wound, and its latest manifestations in the Israeli invasion of Lebanon and the fragmentation of that country, the region suffered from the aftermath of the Shah's overthrow and the establishment of a fundamentalist Islamic regime on one shore of the Persian Gulf. The Iran-Iraq War, pitting Persians against Arabs, and threatening oil exports from the Gulf, had been raging for over three years.

In the north, the Russians had invaded Afghanistan in a move many interpreted as the first stage of a push south to the Gulf and the Indian Ocean. As always, Soviet diplomacy sought to turn Arab-Israeli strains to Soviet advantage. The Soviet Union posed as the champion of the Palestinians, supported extremist regimes, maintained client states in Iraq and Syria, and sold large quantities of arms to all and sundry. Throughout the area recurrent outbursts of terrorism reflected Arab frustrations and the growing radicalization of Arab politics.

Britain, once the dominant power in the region, had divested itself of direct responsibilities as far back as 1968, ending the protective treaties with the Gulf States, in what some condemned as a premature retreat. British interests were now of a more general kind and shared with European Community partners: ensuring the continued supply of oil; doing what could be done to mitigate the effects of the Arab-Israeli feud and preserve regional stability. Individually, we had a strong commercial interest in expanding British exports to the rich Middle East market; here Mrs Thatcher was particularly active, with visits to the Gulf and Saudi Arabia, and the conclusion of the 1985 deal for the supply of Tornado aircraft and related equipment to the Saudi government. Britain retained considerable influence, especially in the Gulf States, where many British personnel still worked. For better or worse, we were still credited locally with special skills and power to guide events, whether directly or through advice in Washington.

At the heart of the region's discontents, the Arab-Israeli issue still resisted the attempts of the most powerful and skilled among Western negotiators to engineer some progress. There had been a break in President Carter's time, with the Camp David agreements of 1978–9 and the Israeli evacuation of Egyptian territory. Then the ice re-formed: there was no thaw on the central question of Palestine, nor any real prospect of one. The protagonists apparently did not want a solution sufficiently to be prepared to make the necessary and painful compromises; and the outside powers lacked adequate means of persuasion.

In this situation Britain and Europe had to be realistic about what they could do on their own. Only the United States could deliver Israel, and even then only with extreme effort and in special circumstances. Britain therefore had no choice but to keep closely in step with Washington and urge movement and flexibility there. Some distancing, some discord even, between Europe and America was possible and indeed desirable. It broadened the Western appeal and reduced the risk of too close an identification with Israel. But such operations had to be carefully calibrated and agreed. The Community's Venice Declaration of 1980, condemned by Israel, grudgingly welcomed by the Arabs, was thought in Washington to be carrying independence too far and came to nothing.

The Americans themselves mounted several initiatives. They all fell between Israeli and Arab stools. Israel would not surrender land for peace and would not admit a Palestinian right to establish a state. Until 1988 the Palestine Liberation Organization (PLO) would not unequivocally renounce terrorism or recognize Israel's right to exist in peace and security. It was not until 1988 that any dialogue was possible between the United States and the PLO.

But in such an unyielding situation it was almost as important to be seen to be trying as to succeed. Movement, or the prospect of movement, was everything. As I saw it, though the West might not be able to achieve the immense feat of an Arab-Israeli settlement, it must at all costs avoid the impression of total stasis and the consequent radicalization of moderate Arab states, leading to renewed fighting.

It was in this area and within these narrow limits that our Middle East diplomacy had to operate. On the whole, I think we did reasonably well. We were in constant touch with Washington and with our European partners. We cultivated our links with the moderate Arabs, particularly King Hussein of Jordan. Between 1984 and 1986 we encouraged him in his efforts to reach a common negotiating position with Yasser Arafat and thereby prompt further initiatives from Washington, though this plan, like so many others, eventually failed.

We also had good contacts with Israel. Mrs Thatcher admired Israel: it was a place where things got done, where operations, whether to irrigate the desert or to storm planes holding hostages, came off. She also had many Jews in her Finchley constituency. After a trip to Jordan in 1985, she paid a highly successful visit to Israel in 1986 and urged flexibility on her hosts. But Israel was hamstrung by a coalition government embracing the two main political parties, and under its rules Shimon Peres was to be replaced by Yitzak Shamir, who did not believe in land for peace or restraints on Jewish settlement of the West Bank. The next year she put to the Americans the idea of an international conference; but they were unwilling to risk a move without a measure of consensus in Israel, which meant in effect giving Shamir a veto.

This modest work to encourage movement was also constantly interrupted and frustrated by the impact of terrorism and Western, particularly American, responses to it. The effect was invariably to polarize the situation and reduce our scope for manoeuvre. For much of the time terrorism was also the obstacle to senior British ministers meeting PLO representatives: the Prime Minister was firm that there could be no such contact with organizations using violence to further their aims.

Some mention of Libyan-related terrorist incidents has already been made in Chapter 9. But there were many other outrages with other authors and sponsors. In late 1983, massive bomb attacks by Hizbollah against American and French military quarters in Beirut forced the withdrawal of the multinational force from Lebanon. In December 1984, a Kuwaiti airliner was hijacked by Hizbollah terrorists and flown to Tehran. Two Americans were murdered. In June 1985, a TWA airliner, with 153 passengers, mostly American, was seized on a flight to Rome and shuttled between Algiers and Beirut, while the hijackers demanded the release of Arab prisoners held in Israel and Kuwait. In September of the same year a group of Israelis were murdered on a yacht at Larnaca in Cyprus; the Israelis bombed the PLO headquarters in Tunis in retaliation. In November an Egyptian aircraft was hijacked to Malta. In September 1986, a number of Jews were shot in a synagogue in Istanbul and an American aircraft was hijacked to Karachi. This does not pretend to be an exhaustive list.

In London we felt we had a good grounding in terrorism. We had to live with the constant menace of IRA attacks; and an IRA bomb at Brighton came near to killing the Prime Minister and her cabinet. We had experienced Libyan methods in April 1984, when WPC Fletcher was shot down.

In April 1986, the vigilance of El Al groundstaff at Heathrow prevented another disaster. As a result, in October of that year an Arab, Nezar Hindawi, was convicted in London of an attempt to smuggle a bomb on to an Israeli airliner. Unusually, there was strong evidence of Syrian government involvement. The policy choice was between expelling the Ambassador and breaking off relations with Syria altogether. I favoured the first because in a full-scale confrontation there was greater danger of British subjects being killed or kidnapped; because with the closure of our Damascus embassy we would lose a key listening-post; and because of the risk to our valuable overflying rights. But the Prime Minister went for a full break in relations and sanctions by our EC partners. She had a good case; but I worried that the imperatives of counter-terrorism were forcing us into an almost Israeli-style isolation, which was not a good position for Britain in the Middle East. And restoring relations was always harder than rupturing them. It took the Gulf War, and Syria's transformation into an ally in that context, plus further tough arguments at No. 10, to get us back into Damascus. Terrorism also meant we had no posts in Libya or Iran.

A further concern in terrorist cases was that the United States might overreact. We understood the extreme provocation; but nothing could have more strikingly illustrated the incongruity between American power and the needs of counter-terrorism than the futile bombardment of Lebanese targets by the US battleship *New Jersey* in early 1984. Following the TWA hijack, a US attack on Beirut airport, which looked in danger of becoming a pirate haven, seemed possible. We saw it as a messy operation, which would identify the US even more closely with Israel, put pressure on Arab moderates and halt the peace process. Britain could easily be sucked in by providing support facilities.

After the attack on the Italian cruise liner *Achille Lauro*, in October 1985, the Americans took action at a more appropriate level. They intercepted a plane carrying the terrorists from Egypt to Tunis and forced it to land at a NATO base in Sicily. The intention was to carry the terrorists back to the United States for judgement; but the Italian government insisted on holding and trying them. The Administration asserted a legal right to respond to state-sponsored terrorism outside the offending nation's territory and by force if necessary. We felt that was straining the law and, as in the case of the raid on Libya, insisted that any action should fall under the rubric of self-defence. But the Americans were right in pointing out that the law had many loopholes, particularly in the definition of piracy.

The sharpest policy, and moral, choices imposed by the terrorist campaign concerned hostages. Increasing numbers of Western nationals, mainly American and British but also Irish, French and German, were seized, usually in Lebanon but also in Iraq and Iran, and held against the release of Arab prisoners or the fulfilment of various policy demands. Occasionally, one or two would be released, then others would be taken. Some were murdered in response to Western action, as after the Libyan raid; others just disappeared. It was a nightmare situation for the victims and harrowing for their relatives. It was also an experience of great frustration for governments, who had to operate largely in the dark, seeking information, endeavouring to bring pressure, but also trying to avoid getting drawn into self-defeating compromises with the kidnappers.

All Western governments proclaimed their unqualified opposition to terrorism. In practice, this opposition was heavily qualified. Some of the weaker brethren allowed terrorist groups to operate from their territory, in the hope of buying immunity. Even among the stricter fraternity covert deals were regularly done. The Germans traded fairly openly; the French went to great lengths in secret, while proclaiming public probity. In order to secure the release of the passengers of the TWA airliner hijacked in June 1985, the Israeli authorities later released some hundreds of Lebanese prisoners; not a simultaneous trade perhaps, but clearly the result of some understanding. To our dismay, the Americans themselves were shown to be enmeshed in the most complex secret bargaining. Britain alone made no compromises.

Here the Prime Minister was at her best. The principle of no deals with terrorists was stated and observed. It could easily be made to look inhuman, or an excuse for inactivity; and it offered no refuge when ministers and officials had to meet the very natural questions of relatives: 'What are you doing to get him out?' But it was right. We could have bought releases, at a high price. And we would thereby have ensured that others would be seized and the price would rise.

This was the painful background to Middle East diplomacy. The foreground was occupied by the Iran-Iraq War. Launched by Saddam Hussein's ambition and folly in September 1980, the war at first threatened to turn into a successful crusade by revolutionary Iran, which would overrun southern Iraq, close the Gulf and subvert the Arab states on the further shore. By 1983 the Iraqi invaders were forced back within their own borders and driven to rely on chemical weapons for their defence. Only Iraq's air superiority and the blockade of Iran's oil exports which this made possible redressed the balance.

The British government had from the outset proclaimed its neutrality and laid down a principle of not supplying lethal equipment to either side, a course which, despite the contrary impression given in much press reporting, was faithfully maintained. We did not want a major shift of power in the region. In private, our comments tended to be of the anxious kind: 'Will Iraq hold out?' Our discussions with the Americans centred on the help that might be needed for the Gulf States. The Iranian threat also had the effect of sanitizing Iraq, drawing it into alignment with moderate Arab regimes and securing help for Saddam from the Arabs, the Russians and some Western countries in the way of money, substantial deliveries of arms, and advice on intelligence, all of which stood him in good stead in his later adventures. For the Americans, with their memories of embassy hostages in Tehran, Iraq naturally appeared as the lesser evil.

Eventually, in 1988, after eight years of slaughter and a million dead or wounded, the massed Iranian attacks petered out. Ayatollah Khomeini, the 'armed imam', said he was ready to accept peace, a decision he described as 'more deadly than taking poison', and admitted his shame before his nation and its sacrifices. In July

1988 Iran agreed to a cease-fire on terms earlier denounced as entirely unacceptable and began to turn to the tasks of internal reconstruction and the repair of its foreign relations.

In the closing years of the war our attention concentrated on maintaining freedom of navigation in the Gulf and securing the uninterrupted flow of oil exports. Successful Iraqi economic pressure, maintained by air attacks on Iran's Kharg Island complex, drove the Iranians into retaliation. They sought to intimidate Iraq's Gulf supporters, notably Saudi Arabia and Kuwait, and to attack their shipping in the Gulf. They began firing Chinese-supplied Silkworm missiles at Kuwaiti port facilities, laid minefields in international and neutral waters and attacked neutral shipping throughout the Gulf, using fast patrol craft. The Prime Minister described it as marine guerrilla warfare. The reasoning behind it was obscure, since it would have seemed in Iranian interests to localize the conflict. As it was, Iranian piracy threatened to be self-defeating, by drawing in the United States in the role of protector of neutral shipping.

In order to deter Iranian attacks, the Kuwaitis cleverly invited the United States and the Soviet Union to charter Kuwaiti oil tankers. The Russians were very ready to oblige: it gave them an opening to a much desired role, that of co-guarantor, with the United States, of Middle East peace. The Americans were wary of a Russian presence in the Gulf, but in the more relaxed East-West atmosphere which Gorbachev had helped create, were not prepared to fight to the death against it. In May 1987, Washington agreed to reflag Kuwaiti tankers and provide US naval escorts for them.

One such tanker hit a mine in July. An Iranian landing craft was boarded by the Americans in September and found to have mines on board. In October American helicopters sank three Iranian gunboats; and a few days later, in retaliation for an Iranian missile attack on another reflagged tanker, the US navy destroyed an Iranian oil rig used as a gunboat base. We were in close touch with Washington throughout these operations and recognized them as carefully measured responses. It seems likely that US firmness, and the unexpected feature of US-Soviet co-operation in ensuring safe passage in the Gulf, increased the pressure on Iran to accept the UN cease-fire terms.

Initially, we were unwilling to join the Americans in minesweeping operations in the Gulf. We feared involvement in what might develop into joint action against Iran. Nor did we wish to be drawn into an implicit alliance with Iraq. From the outset of the war we had maintained a small force at the southern end of the Gulf to escort British shipping, the Armilla Patrol. We felt that should be enough. But in the end, faced with mounting Iranian activity, and US pressure, we joined in and sent two minesweepers. France, then the Netherlands and Belgium, also took part.

The next two years, between the Iran-Iraq cease-fire and the outbreak of the Gulf War, were occupied by concerns of a different kind, foreshadowing modern dangers, namely fears about the proliferation of weapons of mass destruction through the region and the question of responses to this threat. Iraq had had a developing nuclear capacity until, in June 1981, Israeli aircraft destroyed the Osirak reactor on the outskirts of Baghdad. There were now reports of Iraqi progress in restoring that capability and the possibility of another Israeli pre-emptive attack. We and the United States took action to prevent Iraq from acquiring nuclear trigger devices. Components for a super-gun were also intercepted.

In some ways more difficult to handle than the nuclear problem was that of chemical and biological weapons, cheaper to produce, easier to conceal. Syria was known to be strong in chemical weapons; and there were fears that here again Israel might decide to strike first. Iraq was similarly well provided. The Libyans were known to be building a chemical weapons plant; here there could be an American pre-emptive strike and we did our usual contingency work. Most regimes in the area were also busy improving the means of delivery for these fearful weapons, and missile technology, whether from Chinese, Russians or Koreans, was in great demand. In April 1987 the Missile Technology Control Regime was signed by the US, the UK, West Germany, France, Italy and Canada, with the aim of restricting the transfer of technology and equipment. The main suppliers were of course outside the net, but it was an essential first step.

Terrorism persisted, though at a somewhat reduced level of intensity. On 21 December 1988 a PanAmerican airliner, flying from Heathrow to New York, was destroyed by a bomb over Lockerbie in southern Scotland. This was probably delayed Libyan retaliation for the raid on Tripoli of April 1986. Again there was conjecture on the American response, though Washington eventually settled for demands for the surrender of the terrorists and economic sanctions.

Terrorism also cut across our efforts to restore communications with Iran. The *fatwa* of February 1989 against the writer Salman Rushdie raised fundamental issues which could not be sidestepped. It also posed specific dangers to Rushdie, of which we had good evidence.

But, on the whole over this period, the Middle East was not at the forefront of our attention. That was elsewhere, in Central Europe and the disintegrating Soviet empire. In the Middle East the old disputes smouldered with no real prospect of resolution; the more pressing dangers of the Iran-Iraq War were over; and the two contestants, we supposed, would now be preoccupied with recuperation and reconstruction. This convalescent period, we thought, could last quite a while. But here, as so often in the area, we were to be unpleasantly surprised.

19

The Gulf War:
Resolution Rewarded

Iraq emerged from the Iran-Iraq War the winner on points, by a narrow margin, and that thanks largely to outside infusions of money and arms. Its economy was much damaged; but it possessed a powerful and by now battle-hardened military machine, and oil reserves second only to those of Saudi Arabia. It also had an ambitious and reckless ruler in the person of Saddam Hussein. The regime was brutal, even by local standards: it had used gas against Iran and internally against the Kurds. It was also doing its best to acquire weapons of mass destruction via an extensive international procurement network.

These unendearing qualities were known to us. They were not unique in the Middle East. They made the Iraqis a threat, though not an immediate danger. At the same time the country remained an essential part of the regional balance. It was still aligned with moderate Arab regimes, the status quo forces that had withstood the revolutionary Iranian onslaught, and, by way of those regimes, with the United States. And the United States still gave priority to the containment of Iran and saw advantage, both bilateral and for the Middle East peace process, in improved relations with Baghdad.

Iraq stood in great need of reconstruction and offered a rich market to Western businessmen. We, though not all our allies, maintained an embargo on weapons sales. There was strong competition for orders. There were British subjects to be looked after, including some in trouble with the authorities. The usual mix of considerations determining overall policy towards a state in the Middle East applied.

The Joint Intelligence Committee studied the Iraqi procurement network with interest and in early 1990, looking further ahead, saw the country as a potential predatory power, whose eventual victims might be Kuwait or Syria. But no time-scale was set for this development; as always with Saddam, timing was the problem.

What was not so clearly discerned was that Iraq was moving away from friendship with moderate Arab governments and preparing a bid for regional dominance. By February 1990 Saddam was publicly lamenting the collapse of the Soviet Union as a countervailing force to the United States in the Middle East and warning of the extra power this would confer on Israel and the new dangers it would pose for Arab oil. Rather than seeking to draw closer to the United States, as might have seemed logical in such a situation, he began bidding for leadership in the Arab world on a populist, anti-American platform. Publicly he belittled American resolution, pointing to the retreat from Lebanon in 1984 after the death of a few marines; and he may genuinely have believed that American intervention against him could be discounted. Clearly, he saw opportunities in the post-war situation; and the absence of any plausible Arab-Israeli peace process during the critical months of 1990 meant there was one less restraining factor.

There were also pressures on him. Economically, Iraq was in trouble. There were heavy debts. The wartime loans from friendly Arab states were no longer forthcoming; and, partly because of high production levels elsewhere in the Gulf, oil prices were low. Rather than retrenching on his ambitious military expenditure, which would have been the sensible course, he chose to make demands on Saudi Arabia and Kuwait for more money and for higher oil prices. At some point, still unidentified, he decided he would go further and seize Kuwait, with its vast oil and currency reserves, thereby fulfilling an old Iraqi territorial claim and putting his country in a commanding position in the Gulf and the region as a whole.

This was the background to the crisis which burst upon us in late July 1990. The invasion of Kuwait on 2 August brought the Middle East sharply back from the sidelines to the centre of world attention; it posed a direct challenge to regional, and world, stability; and it elicited a rapid and united response from the West and most of the Arab world, which for a short time held out a beguiling but deceptive vision of a new international order under American leadership.

The crisis developed, with some speed, in the last two weeks of July. The detailed Iraqi demands, as set out in a letter to the Arab League Secretary on 15 July, were for Saudi Arabia and Kuwait to write off the loans they had made to Iraq during the Iran-Iraq War, some billions of dollars; for Kuwait to provide a further $10 billion in aid; for OPEC to push oil prices up to $125 a barrel; for Kuwait to yield two islands controlling access to the Iraqi port of Umm Qasr; and for Kuwait to pay $2.4 billion for oil taken from the Rumailah oilfield (a disputed field on the Kuwaiti-Iraqi border).

This was extreme blackmail; and at an earlier meeting of the Arab League Iraq did not dissent from the description. But the terms were subject to negotiation and there seemed good prospects that the Kuwaitis, as usual in such cases, would be able to buy themselves out of trouble. It was agreed that a round of discussions between Iraq and Kuwait under Saudi auspices would take place in Jeddah on 28 July (the date was later postponed to 1 August); and the Iraqis talked of a further meeting in Baghdad. Arab leaders conferred. It seemed likely that the conventions would be observed. Though the concept of Arab unity had become a highly elastic one, a full-scale attack by one Arab state on another was still seen as beyond the pale. Saddam gave countenance to this view by successive personal assurances to King Fahd, President Mubarak and the US ambassador that hostilities were not intended. Arab advice to Washington was 'Leave us to sort things out.'

In the week beginning 23 July we began to get reports of considerable Iraqi troop movements toward the Kuwaiti frontier. By the end of the week there were 100,000 assembled. This naturally raised questions as to Saddam's intentions, despite his professions of peace. We had no means of reading his mind, if indeed he had reached any conclusion by then. Sabre-rattling in support of his monetary demands was the obvious explanation. But the troop concentrations were large and a range of further objectives could lie behind the immediate blackmail: a partial invasion, perhaps seizure of the Rumailah oilfield or the two islands; or a full-scale invasion; or all three in ascending order. And on what time-scale? The Jeddah negotiations, with the prospect of later talks in Baghdad, suggested a gradual approach. But no one could be sure.

Our first assessment, by the Middle East Current Intelligence Group, favoured money as the immediate objective with the possibility of violence further down the line. In their discussion of the paper on 26 July the JIC took a rather gloomier view. I agreed and was getting worried. The next day I sent a minute to the Prime Minister, saying that though the immediate Iraqi aim might be blackmail, it would not stop there. We must expect at least limited military action before long. Saudi backing for Kuwait would not be enough to deter Saddam; and the emergence of a successful predator in that part of the world would be extremely dangerous for Western interests. Britain could do little on its own; and the Americans were sending Baghdad ambivalent signals. We needed collective action. We should speak urgently with Washington and our European partners, with the aim of sending warning messages to Iraq. We should also speak to the Russians and raise the matter in the United Nations.

I received no reply to this advice. But I am sure that the Prime Minister would have sent an urgent message to President Bush if it had not been for the accident of her travel plans: she was scheduled to meet him within days in any case, at Aspen, Colorado, on 2 August. Sadly, she was anticipated by a few hours by Saddam, who invaded at 2 a.m. on the 2nd. The day before, in Jeddah, his delegation at the talks had proposed that the discussions should be suspended and resumed on 6 August in Baghdad. They had then gone off to Medina to pray ostentatiously at the tomb of the Prophet. The negotiations had been an elaborate charade.

The Prime Minister's trip to Aspen may have meant lost warning time; but it certainly accelerated the Western response to the attack. She was present to reinforce the President's best instincts, namely that the invasion was a breach of international law which could not be allowed to pass. She was in her element in such a situation: here was a clear-cut example of aggression, demanding a vigorous, unambiguous response. If Kuwait was lost, no small state was safe. Nor was it just a matter of Kuwait: Saudi Arabia was under threat; and the Gulf States. Saddam could blackmail us all.

These arguments were necessary, not only to dissipate any initial American hesitations but also to counter the inevitable Arab reaction, that the West should stay calm and allow the Arabs to handle the crisis, a course which could all too easily have resulted in supine acquiescence in the new situation. The Prime Minister also added her advice that there had to be collective action imposing a full trade embargo on Iraq. In telegrams to her I had been recommending naval action to blockade the outlets from the oil pipelines leading from Iraq to Ceyhan in Turkey on the Mediterranean coast and to Yanbu on the Saudi Red Sea coast, as well as action to cut off oil shipped down the Gulf from Kuwait. This was the only way to strangle Iraqi exports. At that stage we were doubtful whether the Saudis and Turks would be prepared to risk loss of revenue and Iraqi retaliation by closing the outlets themselves and thought they might welcome outside assistance. As it turned out, they readily took on the responsibility. King Fahd also proved very robust not only in demanding firm action against Saddam, but also in accepting the influx of Western forces that was a precondition for such action.

The war therefore began with the closest co-operation between Britain and the United States, and this led on naturally to joint planning and co-ordination of our military action. Britain offered an armoured brigade to the allied forces and in November increased that contribution to an armoured division, over 30,000 men. The process of US-UK military and intelligence consultation moved smoothly up several gears. This was a situation we were both familiar with and for which our arrangements were tailor-made.

In London a small War Cabinet was established, consisting of the Prime Minister, the Foreign and Defence Secretaries (Douglas Hurd and Tom King), the Attorney-General (Patrick Mayhew), the Energy Secretary (John Wakeham) and the Chief of Defence Staff (Sir David Craig). Along with the Cabinet Secretary and one or two other senior officials, I attended in my capacities as Foreign Policy Adviser and JIC Chairman. The practice was to meet most mornings at about 10, by which time the overnight assessments and the policy papers would be ready and circulated.

The immediate strategic tasks were to ensure the security of Saudi Arabia and build up allied forces there and in the Gulf States; to institute a tight embargo on Iraqi trade; and to obtain the necessary authority for such moves from the United Nations Security Council.

There was also the need to construct as broad an anti-Iraqi alliance as possible; and in the recruiting and management of this heterogeneous coalition President Bush and Secretary Baker, not to mention King Fahd, displayed much skill and resolution. Eventually twenty-four Muslim states were enlisted. Egypt and Morocco were quick to send troops. Nothing was to be expected of Yemen, Sudan or Libya. King Hussein was a deep disappointment and was personally berated by the Prime Minister when he called on her in London. Arafat and the PLO made the mistake of siding with Saddam. But Syria was ready to be won over, and even make a military contribution, for a price, in the form of Saudi aid. Iran stood to one side as *tertius gaudens*, exploiting Saddam's predicament and extracting major Iraqi territorial concessions.

The Turks did not provide troops, but did something more useful by massing on the Iraqi frontier. They also played a key role in closing the Iraqi pipeline and providing bases for allied air operations over northern Iraq.

At the European end of the spectrum, France was able to dispatch a powerful contingent. But France had close commercial ties with Iraq; President Mitterrand expressed himself unenthusiastic about restoring the Al-Sabah ruling family in Kuwait; and characteristically, on 15 January, on the eve of hostilities, the French mounted a last-minute diplomatic attempt to give the Iraqis more time for negotiation.

But the major task of alliance management for Bush and Baker concerned relations with Moscow. The new East-West *détente* and the growing troubles within the Soviet Union meant that for most of the time the two superpowers were able to act in concert. This was a major reversal of traditional positions in Middle East crises and greatly facilitated business in the Security Council. (China normally abstained.) But Gorbachev was an uncertain ally. Iraq was a Soviet client state, with a friendship treaty, Soviet advisers and large quantities of Soviet arms. Gorbachev was constantly torn between his strategic needs and his regional loyalties. At home, he was also having to cultivate the right wing and the military in an attempt to shore up his position; and crises in the war coincided with Soviet paramilitary outrages in the Baltic states. In consequence, Western messages to him were often an interesting mixture of appeal and warning.

When Shevardnadze resigned in December 1990 and was replaced on Gulf issues by Yevgeni Primakov, with an intelligence and Arabist background, Soviet ambivalence on Iraq became even more marked; and the final weeks of the conflict were complicated for us by Gorbachev's repeated efforts to salvage some credit for himself by acting as mediator and softening the clear lines of allied demands on Saddam.

The first stage in the conflict was naturally the establishment of an effective sanctions regime, or one as effective as loopholes like Jordan would allow. But our assessments were soon making it plain that sanctions would take a long time to bite and would not be able to force the policy changes on the part of Iraq that we needed in a time-frame we would find tolerable. The clear implication was that military action would be necessary to recover Kuwait. Many shrank from that conclusion: a popular theme was: 'Give sanctions time to work.' There was nervousness, particularly in the United States, about the likely human cost of a war. Saddam was known to have half a million men under arms in and around Kuwait. They could not all be eliminated by air-strikes. He could dig in and reckon on imposing a costly war of attrition on the multinational force, with casualties which Western public opinion would not tolerate for long.

There were the added threats of his weapons of mass destruction. I went over to Washington in late October for talks with Brent Scowcroft, the National Security Adviser, Bob Gates, his deputy, and Bill Webster, the head of the CIA. We upgraded our estimates of Iraq's progress with nuclear weapons; even so, as it turned out, we were short of the mark. We knew Saddam had stocks of chemical and biological weapons and had to consider chilling scenarios for their possible use. Again, as post-war inspection proved, we greatly underestimated the effort that had been applied and the scale of his resources. These factors made hostilities much more hazardous and unpredictable. But our two governments were able to convey to Saddam warnings that the use of such weapons would result in altogether unacceptable consequences for him. It was probably taken as a nuclear threat; and it worked. Saddam's chemical and biological weapons were not used.

Despite these varied dangers, the logic for military action, land as well as air, was inescapable. The question was the timing. We were in the cooler season in the desert; fighting in protective clothing in tanks was just possible. But the fasting month of Ramadan opened on 15 March, and after that the weather conditions would be intolerable. In any case, it would prove much harder as time went on to keep a large mixed force in the field. There was therefore an opening between November and March, between the assembly of forces and the fasting and hot season, when a campaign could be fought. But it was brief. The Americans were moving cautiously in their preparations and were determined to assemble overwhelming strength before any assault. They announced further reinforcements on 8 November. When these were in place in the Gulf, time would be running very short indeed.

There was another issue, which much exercised us and on which we were not at one with Washington. Must we have another UN resolution covering the use of force? The Prime Minister thought it was not necessary: we had the right to act in self-defence under Article 51 of the United Nations Charter at the request of the victim, the Emir of Kuwait. To seek further authority would be otiose and risky; we could not be sure what riders would be added to the Security Council authority. And resolutions with expiry dates, such as the Americans wanted, would give too much notice of our intentions and invite Iraqi pre-emptive action.

Secretary Baker thought differently. He had his coalition to manage; and he was almost certainly right. King Fahd, the French and the Russians all wanted a further vote. To keep the Russians aboard Baker was constantly having to add grace periods to our ultimatums. And the crucial vote in the US Senate was carried by only 52 votes to 47. Three votes the other way would have been fatal. The Administration approached the transition to full-scale hostilities with great deliberation; and given the delicate state of public opinion in America, scarred by the Vietnam War, they were wise to do so.

In these uncertainties, and throughout the conflict, we had invaluable assistance from Saddam himself. At the outset, he had fatally underestimated American and Saudi determination, and Soviet acquiescence in US policy. It could be argued that he had ruined his chances by invading Kuwait too soon. Had he waited two years or so he might have had a nuclear weapon, which would have greatly complicated allied calculations. As it was, his intransigence, his mishandling of hostages, his spoliation of Kuwait, his clumsiness with the Russian community in Iraq, all played into our hands. The meeting between Tariq Aziz, his Foreign Minister, and James Baker in Geneva on 9 January 1991, on the eve of hostilities, presented enormous opportunities for muddying the waters and diluting allied resolution at the last minute. So did the later meeting in Baghdad between Saddam himself and the UN Secretary General. Both occasions were poorly handled from the Iraqi point of view. Our special nightmare was an Iraqi partial withdrawal, which would have flung the coalition into disarray and delayed the military campaign, perhaps indefinitely. But he made no move.

One consideration much in American minds and our own was the Israeli factor. It was one of Saddam's main objects to turn the Gulf War into an Arab-Israeli war, thereby splitting the coalition and allowing Iraq to pose as the champion of the Arab cause. His speeches regularly played on the Israeli theme. It was therefore crucial to allied strategy that Israel should stay quiet and, as far as possible, disappear from the screen. Would Israel launch a pre-emptive strike on Iraq, perhaps aimed at nuclear targets? We thought not. But if there were an Iraqi attack on Israel? Here the risks were very much higher.

In the event, Saddam attacked Israel with Scud missiles on the opening of the air war. But, under the strongest American pressure, Israel refrained from action. US Patriot missiles were rushed to the scene and special efforts were made in air attacks on the Scud sites from which the missiles were launched. Politically, this was one of the most dangerous points in the struggle: Israel had always relied on massive retaliation; Israeli involvement would have been fatal to the whole enterprise. Happily, Israeli restraint held. It was helped by the American refusal to provide the identification codes used by allied aircraft to distinguish friend from foe, or to halt the allied air offensive in any area, so as to permit Israeli operations.

The Gulf War, so called, lasted from August 1990 to February 1991. But the greater part of that period was taken up by the application of trade sanctions on Iraq, diplomatic manoeuvring and military preparation. The actual fighting did not last long: an overwhelming air assault by planes and missiles launched on 16 January and maintained without respite for the next six weeks; and a very short land campaign beginning on 23 February, relying on deception and spectacular penetration by armoured and airborne forces. It was all over by 28 February.

The end, as the beginning, was something of a surprise. General Schwarzkopf's offensive had almost surrounded large Iraqi armoured and infantry formations retreating north from the Kuwait area across the Euphrates near Basra. The net was not quite closed when the announcement was made in Washington that the liberation of Kuwait was complete and the coalition's war aims had been met. Sizeable portions of the Iraqi force, including Republican Guard armour, were able to slip out to reinforce the reserve held by Saddam around Baghdad. Another day of fighting would almost certainly have been enough to eliminate them.

It seemed a curious decision and I was taken aback to learn of it when I came into No. 10 early on the morning of 28 February. I had had some inkling of it the evening before in discussion with Robin Butler, the Cabinet Secretary, and David Craig, the Chief of Defence Staff. The CDS had just been talking to Washington and had heard of disquiet there over the Iraqi rout turning into a 'turkey-shoot'. There was a view among the President's advisers that to go on would be unchivalrous.

These seemed curious terms to use in such a context. The coalition forces were engaged in destroying the Iraqi divisions that had invaded and held Kuwait. They had gone to considerable lengths to get into the present position. To fail to finish the job now would be foolish and perhaps dangerous.

This was not an outburst of vindictiveness; it related to the serious issue of our war aims and our objectives in Iraq after the war. We and the Americans were reluctantly agreed that we could not advance to Baghdad and topple Saddam Hussein. We had no UN authority to do so. To attempt it would be to split the coalition and confirm Arab suspicions that the West intended to use the war to reassert imperialist rule in parts of the Middle East. It would involve us in the impossible task of occupying and running Iraq. It could lead to the fragmentation of the country and the destruction of the regional balance. Above all, the Americans, the leaders of the coalition, remembered Vietnam and were totally opposed. It is true that, out of office, Mrs Thatcher lamented that we had not gone on to finish the job. But when she was in office there was no serious talk of that kind, for good reasons.

But, if we could not remove Saddam, we had to fall back on the hope that overwhelming defeat at the hands of the coalition would cut away the basis of his internal support and prove sufficient in itself to unseat him. Here the destruction of his armed forces was crucial. Any successful revolt would have to come from his generals and their realization of the calamities he had brought on his armies as well as the country as a whole. To allow Republican Guard forces to escape was no way to achieve this.

But the decision had been taken and the war was over. It had been a period of intense effort, of great dangers and correspondingly bold responses. It had concentrated our attention on one or two big things and in that sense had been a simplification and a relief. Once the crisis was past the unifying impulse was lost and the international scene resumed its old tiresome complexity.

In terms of British foreign policy, the war had been a return to old values. In a coalition led by the United States Britain had again been the indispensable ally and, after the Americans themselves, the main military contributor. British diplomacy had borne a considerable burden at the United Nations and in the Middle East; but the real focus had been in Washington, in establishing the closest possible US-UK identity in analysis, assessment and planning, in clarifying allied thinking, and in helping fend off the Russians and any others whose intervention threatened to sidetrack our diplomatic and military efforts. We had had to get as close to the Americans as possible. Talking to General Scowcroft in October, I had told him, with the Prime Minister's authority, that he could count on us when it came to fighting; but ministers had to be able to assure Parliament that they had been consulted beforehand and had agreed. There was such consultation; and, as the end of the fighting drew nearer, we thought together about the post-war scene. It was a little nostalgic, like old times.

But the war was also an untypical, if heroic, episode. It was not the best guide to future international crises. Such simple direct challenges were unlikely to be the common pattern. After the revived comradeship and the military successes, the everyday world crowded in, above all the issue of Europe. Mrs Thatcher had lost power during the war. Her successor, John Major, would have to face the unsettled and increasingly difficult question of Britain's relations with the Community. As tension slackened, the pieces on the board would be rearranged in a different order of importance; Germany would again bulk larger in American calculations. Even in the Middle East there would be a sense of anti-climax: after all, Saddam Hussein was still there.

There were risings against him, at first in the south of Iraq among the Shia population, encouraged and assisted by Iran. The rebellion was brutally suppressed, using Republican Guard forces, including some that had just escaped the allied encirclement. The Kurds in the north of the country decided their time had come and also rose in revolt. They too were put down. President Bush publicly expressed the hope that Saddam would be toppled, but at the same time made it clear that there would be no American military intervention.

It was an intensely frustrating experience for the Western members of the coalition. With victorious forces on the spot, they were compelled to watch helplessly as Saddam's troops brutalized large sections of the Iraqi population. Some of the press drew damaging comparisons with Russian behaviour before Warsaw in 1944, when the advance was deliberately halted, allowing the Germans to extinguish the Polish rising. But the logic of allied policy was clear; and there was in any event considerable alarm among our Arab partners at the prospect of Iraq falling into disorder and the possible establishment of Iranian-controlled enclaves.

It was against this background that the idea of a Kurdish safe haven emerged. John Major accepted that full-scale intervention was impossible, but recoiled from the idea of total inaction. Always acutely sensitive to media comment, he saw the damage that could be done to the government's achievement in the area by television pictures of Kurdish refugees huddled on the mountains of northern Iraq and south-eastern Turkey. As he saw it, a middle way had to be found between the prohibition of Article 2(7) of the UN Charter, forbidding all interference in a country's internal affairs, and humanitarian imperatives. Creative thinking was called for. Stephen Wall, his Private Secretary, and I helped him work out a course which was just possible, though it involved inroads on the non-interference principle and depended a good deal on the special circumstances of Iraq and the criminality of its leader.

Under the aegis of a carefully worded UN resolution, the Kurds were encouraged to return to certain areas of northern Iraq under the protection of coalition forces based in Turkey. Iraq was called on to allow humanitarian access to the country's population and agreement was eventually extracted for the placing of a UN police force in the country to monitor observance of the resolution. Every encouragement was given to Kurdish-Iraqi negotiations.

It was patchwork stuff and was constantly opposed or evaded by the Iraqis; but it was better than nothing. It allowed the withdrawal of allied forces, an increasingly urgent issue in Washington and London, with clearer consciences. The arrangements for an over-the-horizon force in Turkey and allied surveillance flights over northern Iraq fitted in well with our longer-term plans for handling Saddam. In the wider context of future UN activity, recourse to the humanitarian lever in order to extend the boundaries of UN involvement was a useful preparation for problems of peace-making and peace-keeping that were to preoccupy the international community in coming years.

The underlying question remained, however: how to deal with post-war Iraq? We had to recognize that Saddam had survived and was probably there to stay. He retained sizeable, though much reduced, armed forces and would certainly seek to rebuild them. He would retain his ambitions, and a repeat performance at some future point was far from impossible. Means had to be found to reassure his neighbours, to maintain long-term pressure on him and prevent him developing his more dangerous weapons.

The instrument for this control was provided by UN resolution 687, ending the war. This ensured a permanent ban on Iraqi arms imports; a continuing ban on oil exports until machinery could be found to divert oil revenues for compensation purposes; a Special Commission to investigate and destroy chemical, biological and nuclear facilities; and a series of review points at which relaxation of controls could be related to Saddam's behaviour. A no-fly zone for Iraqi aircraft in northern Iraq, later supplemented by a similar zone in the south of the country, meant that a third of Saddam's airspace was out of his control.

The Special Commission, which was largely a British idea, was particularly important and, over the next years, in the face of every form of Iraqi obstruction, it was to reveal the alarming extent of Iraqi resources in the field of weapons of mass destruction.

The combined effect of these measures was to keep Iraq in the strictest form of tutelage. As I saw it, our object was to demonstrate, particularly to the Iraqi people, that while Saddam survived, their country would remain a pariah, impoverished and with incomplete sovereignty. But it would be a long haul; and to be effective, the control regime demanded an implausible degree of cohesion and tenacity on the part of the coalition powers.

On the more positive side, the defeat of the Iraqi invasion and the related upset in Arab politics offered new opportunities to tackle underlying Middle East disputes. During the war the United States had rejected attempts to link the Kuwait crisis with the Arab-Israeli issue; but the President held out the hope that when the war was over a new effort might be made.

The circumstances were now favourable. A moderate Arab coalition had emerged which was prepared to act against a delinquent Arab state. The old principle of Arab consensus first, which had put negotiations with Israel at the mercy of the least flexible party, no longer applied. The rejectionist front, all of them supporters of Saddam, was now in disarray. The United States was clearly the dominant, indeed the only, superpower; and the Soviet Union, in deepening domestic trouble and willing to co-operate with Washington, no longer offered the Arabs an alternative patron to play off against the Americans. At the same time, Iraqi missile attacks had brought home to the Israeli government the fact that land and buffer zones could no longer guarantee security.

President Bush and Secretary Baker skilfully exploited this opportunity, brought heavy pressure to bear on the Shamir government in Israel and launched a Middle East conference in Madrid in October 1991 under joint US-Soviet chairmanship. The new process began slowly but led on eventually to the agreements of September 1993 and October 1995 between Yasser Arafat and

Yitzhak Rabin and the peace treaty of October 1994 between Jordan and Israel.

In a narrower context, the new Middle East balance brought benefits by allowing us in Britain to restore diplomatic relations with Iran and Syria and finally recover our hostages from captivity in Lebanon.

20

Yugoslavia:
The Future Casts its Shadow

IF THE GULF WAR showed the West, and the whole international community, at its most organized, resolute and effective, the Yugoslav crisis provided the reverse image, one of incoherence and impotence in the face of a deepening political and human tragedy played out near at hand in Europe itself. The states with power to influence the situation could not agree on the origins of the conflict, the techniques to be employed in its resolution, or the final objectives of their operations. The United States and the European Community were for much of the time at odds; and the Community itself was deeply divided. Coming hard on the heels of Desert Storm, the Yugoslav experience was a grim first lesson in the novelty and intractability of many of the problems of the post-Cold War world, and of the limited resources governments were prepared to commit to their solution. Much of the Yugoslav story lies outside the time-frame of this book; but something has to be said about its origins and our early responses.

It was clear enough that Yugoslavia in its old form was unlikely to survive the earthquakes in Central and Eastern Europe of 1989. Its six republics and two autonomous provinces had been held together by the Cold War, by fears of the Soviet Union and by the skills of Marshal Tito. When that cement was removed disintegration was probable, if not inevitable. It was made more likely by the natural shift away from Communism: local elections in 1990 left Slovenia, Croatia and Bosnia-Herzegovina under non-Communist and ethnically dominated governments and Macedonia under a coalition, with the Communists in the minority. Communists retained power only in Serbia and Montenegro.

The other, and fatal, factor was Serbia's determination to recentralize and maintain traditional dominance in Yugoslavia or, failing that, to carve out a greater Serbia from the loosened fragments of the old federation. In these operations the Serbs had the advantage of a devious and ruthless leader in the person of Slobodan Milosevic and overwhelming military superiority in the shape of the Yugoslav People's Army (JNA), largely officered by Serbs.

The disintegration and accompanying bloodshed had been accurately forecast by the CIA and the JIC. Nevertheless the crisis stole up on the policy-makers when Western leaders' eyes were fixed on the Soviet Union and the Gulf War. The US Secretary of State, James Baker, fitted in a one-day visit to Belgrade in June 1991 in order to meet the heads of the six republics. But Soviet internal strains, Gorbachev's weakening position, German reunification, and the chances of using the Gulf War victory to build peace in the Middle East must have been the issues uppermost in his mind. He is reported to have left Yugoslavia weary and downcast, commenting at the airport, 'And I thought the Middle East was complicated!'

The initial American, and European, impulse, natural enough, was to try to hold the federation framework together. It was clear that in the Balkan context any break-up would be violent; and it was feared, particularly by the Americans, that a centrifugal explosion in Yugoslavia would only encourage similar disorder in the Soviet Union. Moreover the federal Prime Minister, Ante Markovic, had earned a good reputation in the West for his success in repairing the Yugoslav economy. But the June visit came too late for the 'As you were' option to be viable. A vote for Yugoslav unity at that stage amounted to approval for the attempts of the Yugoslav army to crush the secessionist movements by force.

With hindsight it is arguable that very early preventive diplomacy on the part of the West, acknowledgement that secession was unavoidable and immediate deployment of peace-keeping troops could have avoided further bloodshed. After all, in the southern Balkans a UN peace-keeping force in Macedonia, with American ground troops as a component, was able to deter another blood-bath. But this course would have called for extraordinary foresight and decision, as well as diplomatic energies on the part of Western governments which at the time were simply not available.

Despite the wish to cling to the old structures, it was soon clear that Humpty Dumpty could not be put back together again and that the federation was defunct. The issue then became how to analyse the situation. Were there now new states suffering aggression from neighbours, and Communist neighbours at that? Could we talk in Iraq-Kuwait terms, in which case the predominant threat was Serbian ambitions? Or were we still looking at a multi-faceted civil war with no clear lines of responsibility?

These were the questions I raised in a paper I wrote for the Prime Minister in September 1991 in an attempt to prompt a full-scale examination of our objectives in Yugoslavia. I came to the unsatisfactory conclusion that while we were ready to concede that the federation was irretrievably fragmented, we still recoiled from the conclusion that international aggression was occurring. This ambivalent attitude was very much the mood at the time; and, unsurprisingly, there was no general clearing of minds.

The underlying reason was that we did not want to get too deeply involved. As we saw it, British interests were not seriously threatened. A decision to try to restore order would mean peace-making rather than peace-keeping: there was manifestly no peace to keep. It would also mean deployment of massive forces in very difficult terrain for an indefinite period. There would be no domestic tolerance for engaging British troops on such terms in a Balkan equivalent of Northern Ireland. John Major was clear on the point and the military experts were even more wary.

Our allies were equally cautious. The Americans were more inclined to see the problem in terms of Serbian wrongdoing and were later ready to advocate air-strikes. But they were firm that they would not deploy ground troops; and without ground forces no effective peace-making was possible. The Germans, in a more crusading mood, talked of joint action against Serbia; but they were in the fortunate position of being able to invoke history and constitutional restraints to explain why in practice German forces could not be employed. No government was prepared to face full-scale involvement; Bismarck's comment that the Balkans were not worth the healthy bones of a single Pomeranian grenadier was much quoted.

And yet, complete disengagement, in the style of Bismarck or Disraeli facing nineteenth-century Balkan atrocities, was unthinkable. There were well-grounded fears that, unchecked, the conflict could spread and involve neighbouring countries. Western inaction in this instance would constitute a precedent and would send the worst message to potential aggressors elsewhere. There was also a belief in the European Community at the time that the crisis offered an admirable opportunity for the Community to display its ability to sort out European problems and apply a common foreign and security policy. As M. Poos, the Luxembourg Foreign Minister, speaking for the Community, famously remarked, 'The hour of Europe has come.' The media too, with their harrowing television pictures and their implicit refrain, 'Something must be done', made inactivity politically impossible.

The compromise course had to be sanctions, diplomatic pressure for a negotiated settlement, and the provision of humanitarian relief. Britain played a leading role, supplying the chief negotiators at two stages, hosting the London Conference in August 1992, and dispatching large contingents of British peace-keeping troops. But each of these second-best options had its drawbacks. Sanctions reflected the seriousness with which the international community viewed the situation; but the arms embargo, imposed equally on all parts of the federation, conferred an enormous advantage on the Serbs, already in possession of most of the weapons; and the denial of arms for the defence of Bosnia became the most contentious and morally doubtful issue in the whole morally ambiguous saga.

Negotiations, the second component in the compromise package, were Sisyphean, given the deep ethnic hatreds, the inter-mix of communities and the incorrigible duplicity of all local parties. There were innumerable promises which were not kept and cease-fires which did not last. The task was not made any easier by the obvious inability of the outside powers to apply superior force. Lord Carrington probably got as far as it was possible to get. But one of his few levers, the withholding of Western recognition of the independence of any republic until all had agreed their mutual relationships, the principle of 'earned recognition', was destroyed by German insistence on early recognition of Croatia in December 1991. So recognition was granted to Slovenia, to Croatia and then to Bosnia-Herzegovina; and the fighting continued and intensified.

In such conditions intervention in the form of peace-keepers and aid-providers was physically and politically extremely hazardous. Peace-keeping presupposes agreed cease-fires, a willingness to honour them, a readiness to respect the UN presence. In Croatia and Bosnia there were ongoing wars. The result, inevitably, was a series of improvisations and half-way houses, unconvincing attempts to provide safe havens for Muslims, arrangements to save Sarajevo from falling, but without the ability to halt the bombardment. These desperate expedients, the natural results of diplomacy without power, no doubt mitigated the horrors and staved off the worst possible outcomes; but, seen from the outside, they came to look alarmingly like complicity in aggression and destruction. The supply of humanitarian aid was more successful; but, given their limited rules of engagement, the troops deployed to secure its passage became in many cases hostages for their governments' good behaviour; and the presence of allied ground forces complicated the issue of air-strikes and inflamed the debates between the United States and its NATO partners about the best strategy to adopt.

But this is to run ahead of events. By June 1992, when I left No. 10, Bosnia had only recently been recognized and the fighting there was in its early stages. When Secretary Baker came through London in late May the talk over dinner with the Prime Minister was of the siege of Sarajevo, how it might be lifted and the necessary limits to any military intervention. We had seen only the first act in the tragedy and there was much worse to come. Nevertheless, incomplete though the story was, certain conclusions could already be drawn.

First, the great powers had come late and reluctantly to the Yugoslav issue. If outside intervention to prevent a looming civil war is to be effective (and it is by no means certain that in this case it could have been), speed is of the essence.

Second, Europe, for all its initial self-confidence, could not manage on its own. For effective intervention, American political and military muscle was still essential (though it was not until 1995 that it was applied). In these circumstances divisions between the United States and its NATO partners, such as occurred over Yugoslavia, were unaffordable luxuries.

Third, however real the constraints on outside action, Yugoslavia sent a sombre message that international order was not to be taken for granted, that at the local as well as at the international level military strength still paid, and that the great powers were unlikely to commit themselves deeply outside certain narrow geographical limits. We were seeing the emergence of what might be called the new parochialism: the leading states would act to control their 'Near Abroad', in Haiti, Cuba or the Caucasus. Only special concatenations of circumstance, as in Kuwait in 1990, would rouse them outside those limits. That in turn meant a heavy burden on the United Nations, called upon to fill in the gap between states' proclaimed ideals and actual performance and to allow them to express their concern at international disorder at less than the full price.

British policy over Yugoslavia was piecemeal, tentative, unheroic, perhaps inglorious; but it was realistic. There could be no grand solutions. Full-scale peace enforcement was never possible without total American military commitment. This was never on offer. And it is arguable that even such commitment, on a Vietnam-like scale, would have been unable to deliver long-term peace in the Balkans. In which case it was better for world stability for America not to try than to try and fail. Once the ideal course was excluded, we were in the grey region of damage limitation, settling for second-bests, defending the bad against the worse. Britain and British negotiators made major efforts towards tolerable settlements. Even on what seemed the most vulnerable aspect of policy, the arms ban on Bosnia, the arguments against a partial lifting of the embargo were strong. But Western prestige and alliance solidarity suffered. Yugoslavia must have been one of the first instances of Britain siding with Europe against the United States in a major international crisis. The commitment to Europe was such that Douglas Hurd was apparently prepared to sacrifice Lord Carrington's peace plan for the sake of a common front with Germany. This was no doubt a sign of the times, of the direction future policy would have to take. But the later wrangling between London and Washington over Yugoslavia would be costly and would contribute significantly to the decline in the special relationship in the later Major years.

*   *   *

In the summer of 1992 before leaving No. 10, I put a longish minute to John Major, reviewing the international scene and some of the coming issues. As a snapshot of those times it is worth recalling. Perhaps also as a contrast to the introductory piece written for Mrs Thatcher eight years before, in another age and a different world.

The background, as I reminded him and myself (the need for reminders is itself revealing) was one of immense success: the collapse of Soviet Communism; victory in the Gulf; the emergence of the United States as the sole superpower; democracy and the market economy almost everywhere the prevailing wisdom; a more active United Nations, offering the promise of better international order. But these achievements were already overshadowed by Western unease and introspection, by economic recession, by the novelty and elusiveness of the new issues and by the requirement for higher and unaccustomed levels of international co-operation if we were to manage them. Our new problems were of the hardest kind, self-generated, divisions among ourselves.

I saw the first task, in time and probably importance, as the conclusion of the current round of negotiations in GATT (the General Agreement on Tariffs and Trade). We were running beyond the deadline; and failure would have deep political as well as economic implications for the three great trading blocs, the United States, Europe and Japan.

But there was also the issue of US-Community strains in their politico-defence as well as their economic aspects. Western security was in a state of flux. What was NATO's function now that large portions of the threat had fallen away? Yet we must preserve NATO as the only real defence in Europe and the crucial defence link with the Americans.

There were now stronger than usual pressures on defence spending. The United States would probably be driven to further reductions in its military presence in Europe. British defence and intelligence expenditure was coming under ever tighter constraints. But there would be new tasks: we should reckon on having to supply a growing number of troops for international peace-keeping duties; the old convention that Security Council members did not provide forces had gone by the board. Our calculations were further complicated by the two conflicting visions of European defence, that of the French and that of the Atlanticists. We needed to be clear what our priorities were.

I was gloomy about our policy on the European Community. I noted the fashionable view that, with many of our partners in disarray, we had a unique opportunity to set our stamp on Europe. I put little faith in that. The Franco-German axis might be under more strain than in the past, but it was likely to hold. The pressure to deepen rather than, or as well as, widen the Community would persist and the struggle over the future shape and direction of Europe would continue. The main current was not in our favour.

Our relationship with Russia was now equivocal, on the one hand a potential military threat as the possessor of a vast nuclear armoury, on the other a partner, even a client. We had a great stake in the peaceful transformation and development of Russia and the former Soviet Union as a whole and had played a leading part in drumming up Western assistance. But our influence over Russian developments was limited and we must expect a prolonged period of deprivation and turbulence in that part of the world.

The liberated states of Central Europe were a different matter. They were units of manageable size and we were committed to bringing them through the tunnel to democracy and successful market economies linked with the West.

Comment on Yugoslavia was resigned. European policy had been a mess. But we could not have pretended that the federation could be held together or have maintained total detachment in the face of Serbian, or Croatian, activities. Nor, in the local circumstances, could we expect a perfect cease-fire before UN peacekeepers moved in. The immediate and limited question was the form of the British contribution.

Moving further east, I noted the rising challenge of Islamic fundamentalism. Algeria was already under siege and the underlying situation in Egypt was brittle. In coming years we might have to face a North Africa under extremist regimes and large-scale immigration into southern Europe. Immigration, from the south or east, like drugs, and transnational crime, represented a new category of problems and threats.

In Iraq, the task was one of keeping up the pressure on Saddam Hussein with the help of sanctions and the Special Commission. The constraints would be lack of international stamina and American unwillingness to undertake a repeat of Desert Storm. The work would mean a continued, and provocative, allied military presence in Saudi Arabia and Turkey and would underline the importance of the latter in Western strategy.

Iran, with an extremist ideology and nuclear ambitions, was a coming danger. But neither that fact, nor the *fatwa* against Salman Rushdie should prevent us from developing diplomatic relations with Tehran, always with the knowledge that they might have to be broken off in certain eventualities.

The Middle East generally reminded us of the pressing problem of weapons proliferation; and Iraq, where we enjoyed exceptional powers, illustrated the difficulty of preventing a determined Third

World dictator from obtaining and concealing weapons of mass destruction (nuclear, chemical and biological). There were encouraging signs from Russia of continuing control of nuclear missiles; but, given the disorder and poverty there, individual scientists and their knowledge would be hard to police. We must assume that some leakage was occurring. The best hope lay in maintaining as tight international instruments of control as we could manage. Even so, we should recognize that we were more likely to slow down than to halt proliferation; and we should be reflecting on the implications of a world with more states possessing weapons of mass destruction and the means of delivery.

An obvious gap in the system was North Korea, possibly within months of a nuclear device. Here the United States would have to take the lead, but would need China's help.

On China and Hong Kong, we could look back on a successful visit by the Prime Minister the year before to sign the agreement on Hong Kong's new airport. But the arguments on financing the project were not over, as I had been reminded when I was in Peking in May 1992. The Chinese leaders were suspicious of the intentions of the new Governor. The colony's newly elected legislature would be more assertive and probably less realistic than its predecessor. The situation was manageable. But if we wanted to help Hong Kong, continued co-operation with China was a necessity. Hong Kong people knew this. The British media were another matter. But a policy on Hong Kong determined by them would in my view be fatal. The warning was more serious than I realized at the time.

In conclusion, I referred to the assets we had, our leading positions in the Security Council, NATO and, still, the European Community, our close links with Washington, reinforced by the Gulf War, our diplomatic and military skills, our intelligence machinery. To these were to be added the English language, the British Council and the BBC World Service, which we should exploit as the French would if they were fortunate enough to possess them. We had our cards and should play them, but only against a clear-eyed estimate of our capacities and the environment in which we would have to operate. As always, it was 'Know your-self, know your enemies', to which might have been added, 'Know your friends.'

In judging such *tours d'horizon* one has to allow for the art-form: they inevitably dwell more on the problems and threats than the successes; the great mass of law-abiding international behaviour, the areas where our relations are working well, are taken for granted. In this case some of the forecasts have worn better than others. But the paper conveys well enough the circumstances and mood of the time: the uncertainties of the post-Cold War scene, the world after 'the end of history', rapidly clouding the triumphs of 1989–91; the tightening economic constraints; the sense that Britain would have to run fast to stay in the same place; the growing number of questions that could only be tackled in concert with other governments; the continuing wide geographical spread of British interests; but at the core the unresolved issues of Britain's position between America and Europe.

As often happened, discussion of the paper with the Prime Minister was overshadowed by more recent alarms. The news had just come through of the Danish vote against Maastricht. So we sat and talked about Europe, rather than China and the Middle East. Willy-nilly, we had been brought back by events to the centre of Britain's concerns.

Part III

Conclusions

21

Britain Great Again?

IN THAT STRANGE entertainment, the Secular Masque, John
Dryden, looking back in old age on the turbulent seventeenth
century, asks what its wars, passions and revolutions have accomplished. His presiding spirit, representing criticism and laughter,
addresses the deities who have dominated the stage throughout the
action and pronounces his judgement and their dismissal.

> All, all of a piece throughout;
> Thy Chase had a beast in view;
> Thy Wars brought nothing about;
> Thy Lovers were all untrue.
> 'Tis well an Old Age is out,
> And time to begin a New.

It is tempting to reach a similar sceptical conclusion looking
back on the hard, bustling years covered in this commentary. After
all the struggles and the triumphs, what was different? Was Britain's
place in the world transformed, or substantially improved? Was the
way ahead clearer?

To others the same period represents a heroic age, when great
deeds were done, a period whose spirit must be kept alive if the
country is to keep faith with itself.

No doubt the truth lies somewhere between these extremes.

Foreign policy is about power, about getting our way in an

unhelpful world. But power is relative; and it is usually imputed rather than applied: governments act on an estimate of what the other side can do. Influence, or prestige, which has been called the halo round power, normally suffices. And a confident, decisive government, particularly one with some practical successes to its credit, can acquire disproportionate influence, impose its own estimate of itself and, to some extent, live beyond its diplomatic means.

For much of the time, Mrs Thatcher's government was able to do this. It had shown its mettle in the Falklands War and in some domestic encounters. It was not at all shy in its economic or political claims. And it had a formidable spokeswoman. It is not surprising that many countries took us at our own valuation.

Moreover, in the first part of this period at least, the balance of forces in the world was favourable. An administration in Washington bent on reasserting American free enterprise values and restoring American military strength, a heavily armed Soviet Union labouring under a failing economy and teetering on the brink of reform, these represented a fortunate conjunction for someone of the Prime Minister's talents. She flourished in late Cold War conditions. Afterwards, as the ramparts came down and East-West diplomacy lost some of its rigours, she was less at her ease.

As a middle-ranking power, if it wished to shape events, Britain had no alternative but to act on the world in collaboration with others, or by proxy. It did so with great success through the most powerful of proxies during the Reagan presidency. No doubt the Prime Minister was fortunate in finding an American leader who took to her so well. But she deserved good fortune. On any reckoning, she was the most responsive, and influential, of allies; and her ability to develop a personal relationship with the President, not just in British but also in wider international interests, represents a considerable achievement. The two Camp David meetings were cases of British intervention at strategic level, well outside our normal range, in the first avoiding potentially serious divisions within the Atlantic alliance over the Strategic Defense Initiative, in the second fending off dangerous and destabilizing concessions by the West to the Soviet Union. They were both instances of superior judgement and effective persuasion.

These were the most dramatic examples. But British influence in Washington throughout this time was disproportionate, exerted through a common view of the world, close intelligence and defence ties, and sympathy between the leaders. It was always a delicate relationship to manage, for example during the Contra scandal; American intentions were often uncertain and worrying; and there were on occasion open disagreements, as over Grenada and the Siberian pipeline, when the Prime Minister did not hesitate to take up an independent position. But these episodes were set against a background of natural understanding and collaboration; and as a whole the relationship was managed skilfully, to Britain's substantial advantage.

Under President Bush links remained very close, but some of the special intimacy was lost and British influence declined from its high point. The principal factors were reduced East-West tension, the growing importance of Germany and the Bush Administration's interest in European integration. Europe was beginning to cast its shadow; and perhaps the low point was reached in the Bush-Thatcher exchanges over German reunification.

With the call to arms in the Gulf War, Britain was back in its accustomed place in Washington, the major ally and the closest confidant. But the Gulf War was not a good precedent for future international crises: Yugoslavia was a more reliable omen. And UK-US relations, though always close and extremely important, declined markedly in the later Major era.

At first sight, the Thatcher-Gorbachev dialogue looks like the eastern complement to the success story in Washington. Mrs Thatcher came close to claiming that she had discovered, even invented, Gorbachev; her meetings and debates with him were deliberately high profile and added to her, and Britain's, international standing. More seriously, she acted as a conduit from Gorbachev to Reagan, selling him in Washington as a man to do business with, and operating as an agent of influence in both directions.

She had no illusions about Soviet foreign policy and she saw Britain's security as her first charge. She quickly realized the value of the Strategic Defense Initiative in sharpening the strains on the Soviet military budget. But at the same time she saw Gorbachev's potential as a factor for change; in their long exchanges she encouraged his reforms and enlarged his understanding of the international scene; and can therefore claim some of the credit for one of the greatest international transformations since 1945, the liberation of Eastern Europe and the disintegration of the Soviet Union.

On closer analysis, such claims need qualification. Gorbachev was moved by a dynamic which had little to do with foreign friends and everything to do with the internal predicament of the Soviet Union. He would have run his course without a British debating partner. Moreover, like many great reformers, he accomplished more, and something other, than he intended. He worked largely in the dark. And he was, for all his remarkable qualities, a transitional figure. The Prime Minister tended to overlook this and to insist on him as a permanent feature of the scene, with greater control than he in fact possessed.

Inevitably too, after a short period in which she alone did the talking, the burden of East-West discussions and negotiations passed to the United States. The West owes a great deal to the steadiness and skills of American leaders, George Bush and James Baker, and before them George Shultz, in managing the East-West relationship in the dangerous era of declining Soviet power.

So the achievement in Moscow was less than that in Washington. But when all this has been said, it remains true that at these two cardinal points of the international compass British policy for most of the time we are considering was realistic, bold and successful. The collapse of the Soviet empire in Central Europe offered further opportunities, which were seized. The Prime Minister quickly recognized the importance of securing the future of Poland, Czechoslovakia and Hungary, whatever was to happen further east; and her visits to those countries consolidated her role as the herald of free enterprise and free politics. This not only ensured her wider personal fame but at the same time enhanced Britain's diplomatic weight and commercial opportunities.

If we turn to the other major states, China was important to us in geopolitical terms as a nuclear power, as a permanent, if inactive, member of the Security Council and, for much of the time, as a counterpoise to a threatening Soviet Union. If it was not yet recognized as a rising superpower, its potential under sensible management was clearly enormous and Deng Xiaoping's reforms were releasing its latent energies and opening the country to the outside world. In addition, of course, China was of critical importance to Britain in the Hong Kong context. It was therefore a demanding and highly sensitive relationship. In this period it was successfully managed. In the wake of the Hong Kong Joint Declaration of 1984 we established excellent bilateral links and, despite the strains imposed by Tiananmen in 1989, were able to keep the channel in good working order and maintain a constructive dialogue with Peking on the future of the colony and wider issues.

Relations with the other great power centre, Japan, were dominated by questions of finance and trade. In general terms, the problem was the Japanese trade surplus with Western countries. At a bilateral level, it was a matter of persuading the Japanese to remove the complex and elusive barriers facing British exports and encouraging Japanese investment in the United Kingdom. Mrs Thatcher applied herself to these tasks vigorously and to some effect, so much so that Japan became one of our best markets and the Japanese came to see Britain as their trade bridge into the European Community. Japanese officials would worry sometimes that their masters' inward and allusive style would not go down well with the Prime Minister. I told them not to worry: when it came to exports of Scotch whisky and British seats at the Tokyo stock exchange, she was interested in substance not style; and the oddly assorted pairs in fact got along very easily.

There is of course always a high degree of continuity in foreign policy, whatever a government's professions; and it can be argued that any British Prime Minister would have undertaken the same task. But in this case, and throughout her trade promotion activities, in South-east Asia and the Middle East as well as in the Far East, the strength of the Prime Minister's personality and the international reputation she had acquired gave extra leverage to her persuasions.

There was another aspect to the Anglo-Japanese dialogue: in common with the United States, we were engaged in persuading the Japanese to take on an international political role more in keeping with their economic strength. We made some progress in this. From the early days we kept the agenda at prime ministerial meetings as broad as possible. The Japanese for their part came to recognize that the exclusive US-Japan relationship was no longer enough and were ready to turn to Europe, particularly Britain, to supplement it. This was not a dramatic relationship; and it was a good deal less important, as well as less abrasive, than its US-Japanese equivalent; but it concerned a leading international actor; and it played its part in strengthening international stability as well as furthering our commercial interests.

This was the wider stage. In narrower contexts, in tackling the thorny legacies of the colonial past, the government again, in the end, acted with realism and flexibility. Tough postures were taken up at the outset and maintained for a while; they expressed the Prime Minister's instincts and they brought their negotiating dividend. But they were not allowed to bar eventual sensible compromises, which reflected an accurate estimate of British power in each context.

On these issues there were, particularly in the early years, happy marriages of prime ministerial will and professional advice. Over Rhodesia, Lord Carrington was able to persuade her to look beyond the Muzorewa government, organize the Lancaster House Conference and impose a new constitution on all the participants. Over Hong Kong, she was induced, after much effort, to abandon her initial embattled stance and accept that a solution could only be negotiated within the tight framework imposed by the expiry of the lease and Chinese determination to recover both sovereignty and administration. The result was a treaty ensuring the colony the most complete protection possible in the real world for at least fifty years after the hand-over. It was generally acknowledged that no better solution could have been achieved. Unfortunately, in this instance the effects were partially undone by a later change of policy under John Major, which his predecessor, reverting to her instinctive approach to the Hong Kong issue, too readily endorsed.

A similar pragmatism was shown in the Anglo-Irish agreement of 1985. This was based on an implicit bargain, on the one hand a say for the Dublin government in the affairs of Ulster, on the other greater security co-operation between the two governments against the terrorists. It proved a disappointing bargain and the Irish tragedy pursued its course; but it demonstrated a readiness to think afresh and, if need be, compromise on the most neuralgic of issues.

In the Middle East, in the years before the Gulf War Britain played a reduced role with some skill. There was less contention with the Arab world than in the past: there were now no direct responsibilities, no inherited position to defend; and oil was, for the time being, a neutral factor. We kept on friendly terms with both sides. We had good relations with Israel. We worked with the moderate Arab regimes, and also with Washington, doing what we could to promote movement on the Arab-Israeli issue, to avoid further polarization and to avert a slide into renewed war. We also promoted British exports, with some success. The contrary factor here was the high incidence of terrorism, forcing us and the United States to respond and thereby limiting our room for diplomatic manoeuvre.

On South Africa, the government's analysis was sound and the recoil from the emotional anti-apartheid crusade intellectually respectable. But the points were made with unnecessary acerbity. The quarrels with the Commonwealth became a self-indulgence on the part of the Prime Minister, a retreat into her favourite role of 'Thatcher *contra mundum*'. The discussion could have been conducted at a lower level of noise and friction. In the end Britain was lucky: events in South Africa took a new turn, not so much because of British advocacy, strident or otherwise, as because of the emergence of a remarkable leader in the person of de Klerk who, coming from the least promising of backgrounds, nevertheless had the courage and vision to see the emptiness of the system he had inherited and to aim for major internal reform. Once reform began, Britain, because of its record, was in a favourable position to exercise influence and did so to good effect. But we were more the beneficiaries than the engineers of the new situation.

Much of the above analysis is in personal terms: the Prime Minister did this or that, decided in favour of this or that course. This is appropriate because, whatever the origins of the policies she followed, she was able to a remarkable degree to imprint her character and convictions on them and thereby on events. She was able to create the illusion that Britain had wider choices than in fact it had, and that her options were new and different. For her, diplomacy was an exercise in personal will. In common with other charismatic leaders, she believed that human determination and energy could move mountains. She was a great voluntarist, an exponent of the heroic view of history, of events shaped by great men and women, the view that Tolstoy disliked so much.

But in the end there is a limit to what the individual will can achieve. The Italian Renaissance writers on statecraft, who described 'what men do, not what they ought to do', drew a distinction between *Virtù* and *Fortuna*. The first represented the qualities of courage, resourcefulness, skill and intelligence which the ruler brings to bear on the blind forces opposed to him, the vagaries of *Fortuna*. History is formed by the interaction of the two. Machiavelli thought the ruler might prevail half the time. Guicciardini, who took a colder view of human affairs, put the success rate much lower.

Mrs Thatcher had *Virtù* in abundance. But *Fortuna* was not always kind and always there were the constraining facts of Britain's objective situation, a small island off the north-west coast of Europe, with limited resources, a glorious but imprisoning past, an uncertain future and a host of economic problems – a weak manufacturing base, low investment, poor education and training among them. It was true that in her earlier years in office she had tamed the unions, made industry leaner and more efficient, deregulated and privatized, creating a new climate of competition and confidence.

But by 1989 the economy was in trouble again and, despite undoubted successes, the country was stuck halfway down the European wealth league, whether above or below Italy a matter for debate. The overall position had not dramatically changed. For such a country personal successes could be transient, co-operative policies were a necessity; and, if adequate influence on the outside world was to be assured for the future, membership of some larger grouping was almost inevitable.

It is here that we come to the weaknesses of British foreign policy in the years in question. They relate mainly to the critical area of Europe.

The opposition to early German reunification was the single most spectacular misjudgement. It reflected a lack of imagination, an inability to appreciate the forces impelling the West German leaders to seize the hour; and a lack of realism, a refusal to come to terms with the situation and accept British inability to control events. It did much unnecessary harm. Again, it was highly personal, an image of the Prime Minister's character, her strengths and limitations.

But the German error was symptomatic of a wider failing, affecting our dealings with Western Europe as a whole. Britain was no longer blind to Community matters, as had been the case for so much of the post-war period. But it was generally unreceptive, suspicious or hostile. I had suggested in my first memorandum to the Prime Minister that, if the United States represented the present, Europe stood for the future. But Europe was not treated as if it was truly our future, rather as if it was a threat, or an adversary. Apart from a short positive spell at the time of the Single European Act, the Community was cast in the role of an antagonist in an increasingly sharp confrontation, first over the issue of our contributions, later, and much more seriously, over monetary and political union. Public opinion, which at the time of the 1975 referendum had been clearly pro-European, and was still inclined to give Europe the benefit of the doubt, was encouraged in Eurosceptic or Europhobic attitudes. The positive case was rarely made.

As so often, the Prime Minister worked herself into her

favourite adversarial position, her perceived opponents being virtually all our natural partners and fellow treaty members. By the
time she fell, she was uttering a resounding 'No' to any further
steps towards European union. Her successor was able to recover
some ground and keep British options open. But, in the absence of
a clear lead from him, British European policy became more and
more constrained by the gathering Eurosceptic tendency within
the Conservative party and the tactical requirements of keeping the
party together. The upshot was that, as the Community pressed on
and the stakes were steadily raised, Britain came closer to finding
itself on the outside of a monetary union which could rapidly
become a European superstate.

Admittedly, there could be no assurance that such a union would
succeed. But, given the commitment of those directly concerned,
the chances were that it would, in which case Britain, on its fringes
only, would be seriously exposed. And if it did not, Britain would
suffer at least as much as others in the resulting turbulence and the
relapse of Europe into conditions reminiscent of the 1930s.

The qualities, or deficiencies, that led to this dangerous situation
need identification. There was throughout the old failure of
imagination, that besetting weakness of British foreign policy, the
expectation that foreign governments would, or should, feel and
reason as we do. At the end of the eighteenth century, commenting
on British policy towards France and Spain, Burke remarked that
'nothing is so fatal to a nation as an extreme of self-partiality, and
the total want of consideration of what others will naturally hope
or fear'.[19] At the end of the twentieth century in the Community
context, self-partiality expressed itself as a continuing inability to
appreciate the strength and the political nature of the drive for
greater European unity, and the enduring force of the Franco-
German axis at the centre of that movement.

As a consequence, the British concept of a Europe of sovereign,
co-operating states was rapidly outmoded and became less and less
of a practical option. The question for Britain was not the abstract
one of whether a Gaullist or an integrationist Europe was the ideal
form. It was, given a Europe rapidly moving towards tighter mone-

tary and eventually political unity, what was the best course for Britain? This question was never thoroughly addressed.

But there was a further failing. Behind the British attitude lay a faulty assessment of the world and Britain's place and capacities within it. With this went a faith in British exceptionalism. It was too readily assumed that this country was exempt from the normal laws governing political and economic success, that we could survive and prosper outside a wider European grouping. The limitations on sovereignty, the threat to the currency, the illusory nature of independence in such a situation were insufficiently recognized. The American connection was too readily overvalued. The ease of communication, the successes achieved in partnership with the United States, nurtured the delusion that Britain could manage with a good line to Washington and little else.

What this overlooked was the hard-headed, unsentimental nature of America's appraisal of its allies. We would be valued for what we could provide, especially in Europe. We tended to see America and Europe as exclusive choices. But this was not how the Americans saw it. In Washington Germany was highly regarded because it was the most powerful country in Europe. And in a farewell speech in 1994 the retiring American Ambassador to London, Ray Seitz, a wise and good friend of Britain, reminded us that our influence in Washington would depend on our influence in Europe. He was merely repeating what American leaders had been telling us for some twenty years.

In the final analysis, Britain had performed impressively on the larger world stage, had cut a figure and for a time 'punched beyond its weight'. These were not nugatory achievements; and at the time they bulked large. But in the longer time frame they dwindled and became ephemeral triumphs. Nearer home, in the area critical for our future, we were distinctly less successful. In Europe, in the eight years covered by this commentary, time was not well used. There was too much confrontation, too much emotion, too much self-indulgence, too little realism. The hard choices were not thoroughly explored, no credible future for the country established. At the end of the period Britain was more isolated than before and in danger of repeating once again, and with much higher stakes, the errors of the 1950s and 1960s. To put it at its lowest, and to disregard the relative merits of the pro- and anti-European cases, on the foreign policy issue most important to their future government and country were deeply divided about the course to follow. In such a state of disarray, how could Britain hope to secure its objectives? We did not even know what we wanted.

It is usual to discuss foreign affairs in terms of interests; and to say of this or that policy that it serves British interests has a fine conclusive ring. But in fact the phrase is little more than shorthand for whatever course has seemed important to our political leaders at a particular time. In his celebrated statement of 1848 Lord Palmerston reminded the House of Commons that Britain had no permanent allies or enemies; only British interests endured. But in fact, at any other than an extreme level of generality, British interests are not, as he claimed, 'eternal and enduring'. They have varied greatly from one epoch to another. At one period they included prevention of Russian access to Constantinople and the Straits. At certain times they have demanded the defence, at others the abandonment, of our position in the Persian Gulf. There is, admittedly, a central core of objectives to which all governments subscribe: British security, British prosperity are uncontentious. But how to acquire and retain these blessings is another matter. It is here that differences arise. And the nearer to home the area of dispute, the greater the incoherence in policy, the greater the danger of failure.

At the time of writing (1996) the arguments and uncertainties over policy and interests run very close to home. Britain has no very clear idea of itself and its place in the world and no clear strategy in mind. Much of this confusion is no doubt due to developments since 1992: the disarray and angry faction have grown. But the seeds were sown much earlier and a significant responsibility lies in the time covered in this commentary, in the failure, in that long period under a government of great authority, to lay the ghosts of the past, set a constructive course on Europe and engage public opinion in its support.

This is a harsher judgement than I should have liked on years where I carried some marginal responsibility and where, in other areas of foreign policy, much was achieved. To make it is in no way to decry those achievements, though it is to place them in perspective. Nor is it to overlook the difficulty for leaders struggling with the huge tide of current events if they seek to look beyond the moment and set a course that is far-sighted and perhaps unpopular. But those are, after all, the pains and privileges of leadership.

The purpose of history, we are told, is 'to urge the mind to aftersight and foresight', to instruct us by reference to what has gone before, so that we do not repeat, or persist in, old errors. We insist on this didactic role since otherwise we are prisoners of the past, and its study is no more than Coleridge's 'lantern on the stern, which shines only on the waves behind us'. Governments of course are not given to learn in this way, or indeed to admit to errors of any kind. Nevertheless, a balanced review of our actions, misguided as well as effective, in what was one of the most exciting periods of modern British history may prove more than merely a private satisfaction. Some useful lessons may be drawn at a time when, as a result of this chequered record, British foreign policy is not just a subject for the writer of memoirs or the diplomatic historian, but a matter of immediate relevance and controversy, imposing present and momentous choices.

Chronology

1979

3 May — General Election. Margaret Thatcher
becomes Prime Minister

25 December — Soviet invasion of Afghanistan

1980

22 September — Iran-Iraq War begins

4 November — Ronald Reagan elected President

1982

2 April — Argentina invades Falklands

5 April — Lord Carrington resigns. Francis Pym
becomes Foreign Secretary

14 June — Falklands retaken

1983

23 March — President Reagan announces Strategic
Defense Initiative

9 June — General Election. Margaret Thatcher Prime
Minister for second term

11 June — Geoffrey Howe replaces Francis Pym as
Foreign Secretary

25 October — United States invades Grenada

14 November — Cruise missiles arrive at Greenham Common

1984

9 February	Death of the Soviet leader Andropov
25 June	Fontainebleau European Council. EC budget settlement
6 November	President Reagan re-elected for second term
15 December	Gorbachev at Chequers
19 December	Joint Declaration on Hong Kong signed in Peking
22 December	Mrs Thatcher meets President Reagan at Camp David

1985

11 March	On Chernenko's death Gorbachev becomes new Soviet leader
16–23 October	Commonwealth Heads of Government meeting at Nassau
15 November	Signature of Anglo-Irish agreement
2–3 December	Luxembourg European Council (Single European Act)

1986

15 April	US raid on Libya
3 August	London Commonwealth summit on South Africa
11–12 October	Reagan and Gorbachev meet at Reykjavik
24 October	Following the Hindawi affair, Britain breaks off diplomatic relations with Syria
15–16 November	Mrs Thatcher meets President Reagan at Camp David

1987

28 March–2 April	Mrs Thatcher visits Soviet Union
11 June	General Election. Margaret Thatcher Prime Minister for third term
13 October	Commonwealth Heads of Government meeting at Vancouver
8 December	Signature of INF Treaty

1988

8 February	Gorbachev announces coming Soviet withdrawal from Afghanistan
2 August	Cease-fire in Iran-Iraq War takes effect
20 September	Bruges speech
2 November	Mrs Thatcher visits Poland
8 November	George Bush elected President
21 December	Lockerbie bombing

1989

29–30 May	NATO fortieth anniversary meeting in Brussels
3–4 June	Tiananmen massacre
26 June	Madrid European Council
24 July	Geoffrey Howe replaced as Foreign Secretary by John Major
22 August	Polish Communists announce coalition government with Solidarity
14 September	De Klerk elected President of South Africa
7 October	Gorbachev visits East Berlin
9 October	Major demonstrations in Leipzig
18–24 October	Commonwealth Heads of Government Conference at Kuala Lumpur
26 October	Nigel Lawson resigns. John Major Chancellor of the Exchequer. Douglas Hurd Foreign Secretary
9 November	East Germany opens border with West Germany
10 November	Demolition of Berlin Wall begins
2–3 December	Bush meets Gorbachev off Malta
10 December	End of Communist rule in Czechoslovakia
22 December	Ceausescu overthrown in Romania

1990

2 February	De Klerk lifts ban on ANC
10–11 February	Kohl visits Moscow

11 February	Nelson Mandela released
30 May–2 June	Bush and Gorbachev meet in Washington and at Camp David
6 July	NATO summit in London
16 July	Kohl meets Gorbachev at Stavropol
2 August	Iraq invades Kuwait
3 October	German reunification
27–28 October	Rome European Council
1 November	Geoffrey Howe resigns
19–20 November	Treaty on Conventional Forces in Europe signed in Paris
28 November	Margaret Thatcher resigns. John Major becomes Prime Minister
20 December	Shevardnadze resigns as Soviet Foreign Minister

1991

16 January	Gulf War. Air attacks on Iraq begin
23 February	Ground assault in Iraq
27 February	President Bush announces liberation of Kuwait
12 June	Yeltsin elected President of the Russian Federation
25 June	Slovenia declares independence
26 June	Croatia declares independence. Fighting in Yugoslavia
18–21 August	Coup against Gorbachev fails
23 August	Russian Communist Party activities banned
30 October	Madrid Conference on Middle East opens
1 December	Ukraine votes for independence
8 December	Yeltsin and leaders of Ukraine and Belarus declare Commonwealth of Independent States
9–10 December	Maastricht Conference
23 December	German recognition of Slovenia and Croatia. Other EC governments follow in January 1992

25 December   Gorbachev resigns

1992

22 February   UK decides to send 1,000 troops as part of
                          UN peace-keeping forces in Croatia

3 April   EC recognition of Bosnia

7 April   US recognizes Slovene, Croat and Bosnian
                          independence

9 April   General Election. John Major Prime Minister
                          for second term

2 June   Danish referendum rejecting Maastricht

Notes

1. Percy Cradock, *Experiences of China* (John Murray, 1994).
2. Article in R.W. Seton-Watson and George Glasgow (eds.), *The New Europe*, 1919 edition, quoted in Gordon Craig and Felix Gilbert (eds.), *The Diplomats, 1919–1939* (Princeton University Press, 1953), Vol. 1, p.21.
3. H.A.L. Fisher, *A History of Europe* (Edward Arnold & Co., 1936), Preface.
4. Henry Kissinger, *The White House Years* (Weidenfeld & Nicolson and Michael Joseph), p.54.
5. Noel Annan, *Changing Enemies* (HarperCollins, 1995), p.60.
6. Paul Kennedy, *The Realities behind Diplomacy* (George Allen & Unwin, 1981), p.262.
7. Margaret Thatcher, *The Path to Power* (HarperCollins, 1995), p.88.
8. *Financial Times*, 23 March 1985.
9. Henry Kissinger, *Diplomacy* (Simon and Schuster, 1994), p.783.
10. Alexis de Tocqueville, *La démocratie en Amérique* (1835 and 1840: trans. David Campbell Publishers Ltd., 1994), Vol.1, p.235.
11. Mikhail Gorbachev, quoted in *Pravda*, 26 June 1987.
12. Mikhail Gorbachev, quoted in *Pravda*, 15 July 1987.
13. Nikolai Shmelyev, in *Novy Mir*, quoted in Robert G. Kaiser, 'The USSR in Decline', *Foreign Affairs*, Spring 1988.
14. Robert M. Gates, *From the Shadows* (Simon and Schuster, 1996), p. 381.

15. Gates, *op. cit.*, p. 381.

16. Alexander Yakovlev, quoted in *Washington Post*, 16 September 1991.

17. Quoted in Roy Denman, *Missed Chances* (Cassell, 1996), p.198, and in Charles Grant, *Delors* (Nicholas Brealey, 1994), p.62, who in turns draws on Jean François Deniau, *L'Europe Interdite* (Editions du Seuil, 1977). There is some uncertainty whether Russell Bretherton, the British representative, used these precise words which, for him, have an over-rhetorical ring. But his sentiments and his withdrawal were certainly approved by the British government.

18. Robin Renwick, *Economic Sanctions* (Harvard Studies in International Affairs, 1981), p.92.

19. Edmund Burke, *Remarks on the Policies of the Allies with Respect to France, 1793* (George Bell & Sons, 1906), Vol.III, p.440.

Index